Literary
Reviewing

Literary Reviewing

Edited with an Introduction by
JAMES O. HOGE

University Press of Virginia
Charlottesville

THE UNIVERSITY PRESS OF VIRGINIA
Copyright © 1987 by the Rector and Visitors
of the University of Virginia

First published 1987

Library of Congress Cataloging-in-Publication Data

Literary reviewing.

   1. Literature—History and criticism—Theory, etc.
2. Book Reviewing. I. Hoge, James O. II. Title.
PN441.L487 1987   808'.066028   87-8309
ISBN 0-8139-1146-X

Printed in the United States of America

Contents

James O. Hoge

Introduction

As recently as the first half of the eighteenth century there was no regular outlet for what we have come to know as book reviewing. In 1749 the Monthly Review in London began to publish analyses of recently published works of fiction, and the rival Critical Review followed suit soon after. But it was not until the nineteenth century that works of scholarship received notices of any sort in journals or the popular press, and even as late as the beginning of this century more often than not to "review" a written work meant to assess a new novel, drama, or volume of verse. To be sure, authors have always quarreled and have often done so in print, but the systematic reviewing of academic books, usually performed by one scholar looking at another scholar's work, scarcely existed at all a hundred years ago. The spread of literacy, the growth and expanding influence of the universities, and the awesome increase in scholarly publishing itself, however, have created an audience for the scholarly reviewer, and today the evaluation and elucidation of works of scholarship is pursued with unprecedented vigor.

These days many notices in the daily or weekly press or in the library journals appear before the scholar's book has seen the light of day, and a book of any real importance will continue to be reviewed in academic journals for two or three years. One might suppose that Lord Byron, who blasted those who "censure" and lamented the growth of their trade in English Bards and Scotch Reviewers, would be appalled by the present state of affairs. But of course Byron himself "reviewed" nearly all the authors of his day, "from soaring Southey down to grovelling Stott," and insisted he was performing an indispensable public service by so doing. Reviewers, whether they judge scholarship or art, do perform an immensely important function. Books are written to elicit a response, and the scholarly dialogue that reviews instigate is essential to the growth of knowledge. Scholarship loses its raison d'être if it fails to inspire debate and argument, and it is the review more than anything else that ensures the lively and healthy interchange of ideas in any academic field. The scholarly reviewer is in part an arbiter of taste and a consumer adviser, telling the reader which of the new books in his field is worth his time. But the reviewer of scholarly works is also a critic who analyzes a book, explains its argument or its methods, highlights and illustrates its most significant contributions or shortcomings, and initiates its absorption into the whole body of scholarship.

In 1977, when James West and I established Review, an annual published by the University Press of Virginia and devoted entirely to reviews of scholarly work in English and American language and literature, we did so with two primary purposes in mind. We wanted to promote scrupulous and responsible reviewing that would measure up to the most rigorous and exacting standards of scholarly excellence. And we wanted to encourage a reassessment of the purpose and importance of scholarly reviewing. If, as we believe, reviewing is difficult, grueling work that demands intelligence, analytical ability, intellectual humility, and a dedication to the moral imperatives of absolute candor and fair play, and if reviewing performs the essential service of promoting what is good in scholarship while discouraging what is bad, then the intellectual community should regard reviewing just as seriously as it does any other kind of academic work.

For the past nine years Review has offered the scholarly community a new forum exclusively for reviews, a place, previously unavailable, to publish what are really review-essays, discursive, expansive—something like the notices that appeared in the old Blackwood's and the Edinburgh Review, though rather more scholarly and less arcane. Nearly all the reaction to Review, and to the standards we espouse, has been positive. Apparently our attempt to dignify and elevate scholarly reviewing has struck a positive note with many people in the profession. Nothing, I think, has been more appreciated than our relaxation of length restrictions. Traditionally most academic journals have limited reviewers to a narrow space, forcing scholars to work, as it were, in miniature. By giving authors more space we have received better reviews, not just longer ones, and we have been successful in attracting topflight scholars quite readily by offering virtually unlimited space.

Over the years of editing Review, we have engaged in all sorts of discussions about reviewing with colleagues at professional conferences, *with editors of other journals, with our contributors in the process of working with them on their manuscripts. At some point during all that activity it occurred to me that there might be a place for a volume that collected the best thinking of a number of distinguished scholars about the reviewing of literary scholarship. The reaction of our publisher was favorable, so I set about persuading former reviewers who had written particularly fine essays for* Review, *and others whose work I respect, to turn their attention to the subject of reviewing itself.*

While all reviewers of scholarly books must employ certain of the same methods and standards, there is a very real difference between reviewing a scholarly edition, say, and a critical work, or a critical work and a biography. In making assignments for this volume, therefore, I did so by the category of book reviewed, engaging a well-known biographer to do the piece on reviewing biography, a distinguished literary historian to do the essay on reviewing literary history, and so forth. Obviously the compartments are not airtight, and it might be argued that there are more similarities than differences in reviewing various kinds of scholarly books. Certainly it is not uncommon for a scholar to treat several kinds of books in his various reviews—and occasionally even to do so in the same review. And then there is the matter of where a scholar publishes and how that affects his handling of a particular review. A person might write one sort of review for Newsweek, *another for the* New York Times, *and a different kind altogether for the* Journal of English and Germanic Philology. *But perhaps the disparities would be greater if he were examining a biography than they would if he were reviewing a concordance, a handbook, or a bibliography.*

Ralph Cohen confronts the problem of bias in reviewing, especially the sort of negative bias that distorts an author's theories and contentions. Observing that reviewing is never a "neutral enterprise," he is troubled by the inevitable competition, especially apparent in the narrow field of literary theory, between the author of the review and the author of the book he examines. Since a reviewer's own prejudices and assumptions can never be wholly avoided, he must admit or "expose" his own views from the outset. Thus we should expect that the reviewer will stress his own positions in his evaluation of another's work, but he must not fail to acquaint us thoroughly with the ideas of the other author as well, and he must do so as objectively as possible. But how objective can any re-

viewer, any writer, be? The reviewer's decisions about what to write present him with moral problems, not only because he must endeavor to be fair to every book he reviews, whether it supports or attacks his own work and theories, but also because scholarly reviews have come to be one of the chief determinants of advancement or failure in the academy. "It is one thing to quarrel with the arguments of Stanley Fish or M. H. Abrams or Jacques Derrida; quite another to quarrel with the book of an unknown assistant professor." How can a reviewer, influenced as he is by his own premises and by "his concern for the fate of society or for the author's fate or for his own," offer his audience a reliable judgment of any text?

As crucial as his evaluation of the quality, value, and contribution of a book may be, Derek Pearsall emphasizes, the reviewer must first of all provide the reader with a useful précis. "Opinions are ten-a-penny and the pungent phrase a mere gift, but précis is one of the most strenuous and demanding of all intellectual activities." The appraisal of a literary history or any other scholarly work begins here. Whatever else the reviewer does will be worthless without an equitable, accurate, and clear explanation of the book's contents. But what if the contents of a scholarly book are themselves inaccurate, unfair, unclear, cryptic? Stanley Weintraub offers the reviewer of literary biography a series of cautionary tales. Such a reviewer should accept, on faith alone, little or nothing in the life he reviews. A biography, or some part thereof, is often fiction masquerading as fact. The reviewer is very much on his own in attempting to check the veracity of what his author has written. He should first of all ask himself why the book before him was written, and he should be particularly suspicious of "lives written by people with obvious axes to grind."

Angus Easson comments on the challenges presented the reviewer by various kinds of editions of letters, journals, and diaries. Particularly difficult to review, he says, are editions which themselves have little literary merit but which nonetheless are important because of their authors. Hardy's letters, for example, and Tennyson's are largely non-literary documents written by literary men. They cannot be judged on their intrinsic merits but demand that the reviewer show how they function in the context of their author's life and work.

Richard Altick blasts the proliferation of shoddy bibliographies and other reference tools, often unjustly praised by ill-informed or gullible reviewers, and sets down two indispensable criteria which the reviewer should use to judge all such works: inclusiveness and authority. James L. W. West III contends that of the various genres and subgenres of literary scholarship, descriptive bibliography is the most ineptly reviewed. Surely the scholar who reviews a descriptive bibliography ought to be well informed about descriptive bibliography itself. If he is, he will know that there are specific things that the author of every descriptive bibliography must do. If a bibliographer fails to do any of these things, the reviewer should fault him and point out the shortcomings of his book to its potential users.

Two other essayists, Robert L. Patten and Bruce Macphail, look at reviewing from the vantage points of the academic journal and the university press. Patten offers wide-ranging observations about what gets reviewed, why and how, and in which publication, and he warns of the need for both balance and coherence among the reviews a journal runs. He concludes that there are many useful sorts of reviews, including the oft-despised "springboard" review that for the most part ignores the book supposedly under examination in order to advance its author's own theories or interpretations. Such a review, often "more significant for the reviewer than for the work reviewed," may elucidate the reviewer's ideas in such a significant way that it will survive long after more orthodox reviews have disappeared. Macphail explains that reviews not only provide publishers with invaluable evaluations of the worth of what they publish but also serve as the single most effective promotional device for university presses. And he sets down helpful specifics about how publishers can best go about securing reviews of scholarly books.

Finally, Michael West's essay presents a general overview of our subject, addressing some of the thorniest problems of scholarly reviewing. West is particularly concerned with choosing the reviewer and with the ever-present dangers of perfunctory reading and writing, backstabbing, and cronyism. He puzzles over "the classic dilemma of the scholarly reviewer": how to examine books thoroughly and how to establish intellectual credibility without sufficient space. "To improve the quality of reviewing in this profession," he writes, "editors will have to encourage somewhat longer reviews." Concerned also that so little academic credit accrues to scholarly reviewing, West asks that more respect be accorded reviews and reviewers by those involved in personnel decisions. He cautions, however, that if reviewing is to be taken seriously it must at all costs avoid the backscratching and the "booster mentality" that color the critiques of many reviewers and weaken the credibility of all.

Examining its subject from a variety of distinct perspectives, this collection of essays offers insights into both the general nature and purpose of scholarly reviewing and the numerous dilemmas faced by those who practice it. The collection also presents its authors' discernments about how to review particular kinds of scholarly books, what to look for, what to be wary of, what to hold the author accountable for, in this kind of work or that. All those who evaluate scholarly books, whether frequently or occasionally, will find problems that they recognize addressed here. Indeed there is much here of interest to the intellectual community as a whole, involved as it must be with the reviewing of scholarly books. Reviews are invaluable to editors of learned journals, to directors of university presses, to academicians involved in tenure and promotion decisions, to scholars in every field of research and knowledge, to every reader who has occasion to open an academic book. Perhaps this volume, like Review, will promote a widened awareness of the altogether crucial importance of scholarly reviewing.

For a variety of reasons I am indebted for assistance in the preparation of this book to Arthur M. Eastman, Hilbert H. Campbell, the late Walker Cowen, Gerald Trett, and Leota Williams. My appreciation is also due each of the contributors to this volume; and I must not forget to thank James West in particular, for his advice and support as well as for his essay.

Literary
Reviewing

Ralph Cohen

Reviewing Criticism: Literary Theory

1. What Is "Literary Theory"?

Literary theory has joined a host of other subjects that in our time have been pronounced dead: the author, the novel, God, concrete poetry, archetypal and genre criticism. As Terry Eagleton inters literary theory, he finds that from its grave arise the blossoms of a theory of culture. Literary theory, which once seemed the counterpart of scientific theory, has ceased to search for the "method" by which literature could be studied.[1] Like scientific method, literary method has turned out to be a fiction. The need to give coherence to literary study has met with grave doubts about the coherence or unity of writing. And it is not surprising to find the late Paul de Man explaining that he cannot find in his own collection of essays a coherence that would give it consistency and unity.

> The fragmentary aspect of the whole is made more obvious still by the hypotactic manner that prevails in each of the essays taken in isolation, by the continued attempt, however ironized, to present a closed and linear argument. This apparent coherence within each essay is not matched by a corresponding coherence between them. Laid out diachronically in a roughly chronological sequence, they do not evolve in a manner that easily allows for dialectical progression or, ultimately, for historical totalization. Rather, it seems that they always start again from scratch and that their conclusions fail to add up to anything.[2]

Whether or not de Man was a reliable critic of his own work, the point is that "literary theory" is no single-voiced phenomenon. To review "literary theory" in 1987 is not a simple, readily recognized choice; it is, for example, difficult to know whether Eagleton's *Literary Theory* is a theoretical or historical study. It begins with a chapter on "What Is Literature" but has no chapter on "What Is Literary Theory?" Eagleton claims that literary theory is an "illusion." He writes that "it is an illusion first in the sense that literary theory, as I hope to have shown, is really no more than a branch of social ideologies, utterly without any unity or identity which would adequately distinguish it from philosophy, linguistics, psychology, cultural and sociological thought; and secondly in the sense that the one hope it has of distinguishing itself—clinging to an object named literature—is misplaced."[3] Literary theory is, in his argument, a small part of the larger study of "culture." But in reviewing this claim it must be noted that Eagleton assumes that different generic writings have neither unity nor identity. If literary theory cannot "adequately" be distinguished from philosophy or linguistics, it cannot be an independent subject. But hiding behind "adequately" is the basis for distinct subjects. Who, if not critics, determine whether "literary theory" is an independent subject? And is it not reasonable for them to argue that the writings called literary theory can be discussed more adequately as an independent discipline than as part of a discipline called "social ideologies"? The reviewer of *literary theory* may indeed object to the selection of ideology as the chief basis governing such theory. He might, at the very least, indicate the unimportance of the idea of art or pleasure for Eagleton since these are, for him, always subordinated to ideology.

Is "literary theory" a theory of works that fall into the genre "literature" or is it a theory of any work that can be generalized about and analyzed in the procedures applied to poems and novels? Barbara H. Smith and Murray Krieger reserve "literary" theory for theorizing about works that are considered by them to be part of "literature." Paul de Man and Harold Bloom, for example, refer to "literary theory" as a way of theorizing about any text, using the term *literary* to refer to writing rather than to a specialized category of writing. The reviewer will, therefore, point to the concept of "literary" that is being used and note the examples that an author offers of "literary" texts.

When René Wellek and Austin Warren published their *Theory of Literature* in 1949, the book contained a chapter on "Literary Theory, Criticism, and History" written by Wellek. And he made the point then that literary theory, criticism, and history "cannot be used in isolation . . . they implicate each other so thoroughly as to make inconceivable literary theory without criticism or history, or criticism without theory and history, or history without theory and criticism."[4]

It is unnecessary to point out that "scientific theory" in the view of Thomas Kuhn is a term for the way scientists practice their discipline; it characterizes solutions that result from problem solving. And problem solving does not result from one particular "method." So, too, literary theory is not some isolated study despite the fact that some practitioners seem to conceive of it as a purely abstract enterprise. Giving it the kiss of death is usually the result of this separation of theory from the actual study of literary texts. But no thoughtful practitioner of literary theory would want to make this separation. Even F. R. Leavis, who had little patience for literary theory, did not seek to eliminate it but to find the proper (secondary) place for it in literary study; the primary place he reserved for the attainment of "a peculiar completeness of response" to the concrete fullness of the poem: "I am sure," Leavis wrote, "the kind of work I have attempted comes first, and would, for such a theoretical statement to be worth anything, have to come first."[5]

The notion of primacy is, perhaps, a mistake since the interaction between theory and practice is such that simple hierarchizing is misplaced. After all, to refer to Shelley's "Mont Blanc" as a *poem* is to assume knowledge of what a "poem" is, and that is a theoretical assumption, not the result of a completeness of response. And many contemporary theorists recognize this. Murray Krieger, for example, draws attention to this interaction when he declares that each "new work challenges our theory and our theory challenges each new work."[6] Any literary theory as he conceives it generalizes about texts, but since such generalizations are based on past texts they are challenged by present and future texts. Thus theory is challenged by new texts and needs to be rethought and rewritten to accommodate those writings for which it was not intended. Krieger quite rightly discusses the relation between theory and practice. Any theory demonstrates its adequacy by its applicability. Its value lies in its usefulness in helping scholars and students deal with problems that literary texts raise.

Thus far I have been dealing with the ambiguities latent in "literary theory," the last two words of my title. Since texts identified as "literary theory" are passed on to a reviewer, what are the assumptions that govern such a classification and designation? What is it that a reviewer of theory reviews? He reviews any text that is primarily concerned with the nature of literary language, the problems pertinent to interpretation, the nature and kinds of genre, the place of value in literary study, and the construction of systematic statements about relations among the author, the text, society, and other texts. Theoretical texts are intertwined with critical and historical studies so that a theoretical text may be considered a historical text or even a "fictional" text as well. The consequence of such intertwining is that the reviewer will need considerable malleability in describing a theoretical text since its theoretical character cannot readily be identified without specifying a series of interrelations that make it more than one kind of text. One of the tasks of a reviewer, therefore, is to describe the text as a combination of elements involving historical, critical, and other discourses.

II. Readers and Reviewers

When writing a "scholarly" review, the reviewer obviously seeks to familiarize himself with his audience. He seeks to discover, if he does not already know, for whom the review is written. Students, scholars, and critics constitute in large part the audience for theory and for theoretical reviews. Robert Scholes puts it this way: "A substantial portion of the audience for theory is composed of teachers. Teachers read theory in order to 'keep up'—as we say—with the field of literary study, partly in response to the pressure all fashions or modes of behavior exert in this most modish of all possible worlds; partly, perhaps, for the pleasures of concentration and controversy; but also, surely, for ideas that will enhance their performance as teachers in the field of literary studies."[7] One should not, however, overlook those readers of theoretical books and their reviews who disdain theory, and read it in order to parody it. For such readers, literary theory is less a corpse than a clown.

Fashion, controversy, instruction, use, amusement—these are some of the reasons for reading theory and reviews of theory. But review readers do not often read the books under review. Rather they read reviews to discover the issues theorists are raising, to learn about the theoretical books reviewers consider important, to familiarize themselves with different theoretical vocabularies. Moreover, scholars read reviews not only to learn about the books under review; they read them to learn what the reviewer thinks and to familiarize themselves with his theoretical ideas.

Since a reviewer, in describing a text, selectively rephrases it, the reader will look for a description that takes account of the varied writing of theoretical discourses. It is not merely that such discourses combine literary theory with literary criticism and literary history; they also combine it with autobiographical and other writings. The reader is no single entity but a body of more or less knowledgeable responders. Some of these will want an explanation of the consequences of any particular theoretical combination.

Some readers of reviews expect distinctions to be made between an author's use of rhetoric to develop new thoughts and his use of it to shield or support old ones. The review reader knows that the prejudices of a reviewer are written into a review, and he knows this because he is familiar either with other writings of the reviewer or the author or with other reviews of the same book. Since a reviewer's prejudices and assumptions may be minimized but not avoided, the review reader will expect to have them exposed. A reviewer who makes his own views clear by juxtaposing them with the author's reduces the most obvious sources of distortion. But reviewers, like other people, often do not know or recognize their deep-seated prejudices, those that are intertwined in their very style of writing. A reviewer's exposure of his distortions can be revealed in his statements of an author's limits—his claim of what an author is resisting, supplementing, attacking, or avoiding. He exposes his own views in relating those that confine the author, in judging the confinement as reasonable or trivial.

I have been using the terms *reviewing, review,* and *reviewer* in the formal sense of a critical article on a recent book or books that is published in a periodical or other reviewing organ. But the terms *review* and *reviewing* apply to activities that are not published but written and circulated in academic departments, usually to members who have not read the original materials. Such "reviews" form part of academic decision-making. There, as well as in published reviews, the process of reviewing carries within it the assumption of authority and the distancing of the audience from reviewed texts.

So, too, in publishing, "reviewing" provides the publisher with a so-called authoritative decision about accepting or rejecting a manuscript. It is not necessary to point out that "reviewing" grants authority to individuals or groups that is normally vested in those who bear responsibility for decisions. Reviewing as a procedure can easily become the basis for bureaucratic control and the continuance of prejudice. And this is especially the case when those who read manuscripts and those who publish reviews of them share the same views and even the same roles at different times.

Considering the number of books written in any field during a year, the reviewing procedure may seem a reasonable one, but the secondary processing of information that it produces cannot be denied. Reviews may be useful, even necessary, to help readers keep abreast of work in a field, but they often familiarize the reader with the ideas of the reviewer rather than with those of the author.

III. Types of Theoretical Reviews

Any competent review inevitably restates the premises of the author, and even though a reviewer may quote the author himself, he reassembles the argument for the reader. But no review can substitute for the reading of a book. What it does, is indicate what values the reviewer finds or misses in the book. In this respect the reviewer finds himself, whether he wishes it or not, in a judgmental role. No matter how careful he is in seeking to present the book's argument, he has to render it by selection and by his own words. Every reviewer is a writer, and in this procedure he differs from the nonreviewing reader who is under no obligation to write.

The reviewer becomes an author and his own review competes with the book he is reviewing. In this he resembles the authors he reviews. It is not surprising that contemporary theorists are intent upon developing "original" theories. Whether it is Bloom's version of Emerson and Freud, or de Man's particular variation of rhetorical theory or Jameson's Marxist literary theory—all such theorists seek to announce their originality. Reviewing theory very often results in the imitative contamination of originality because the reviewer seeks to match the ingenuity of the author. In such a situation similarities among theoreticians are made to dwindle and differences—no matter how trivial—come to be emphasized.

Since theoretical reviewing is a relatively narrow field, it is especially troubled by the internecine conflicts among the participants. For the reviews are very often written by the theorists who are themselves authors and who in their reviews reiterate the positions they espouse, stressing minor differences rather than major agreements. Thus Eagleton has his Marxism which differs from Jameson's and Lotman's. Other differences rather than similarities are stressed between the writings of French and American psychoanalytical critics, between the various phenomenologists, between the reader's response theorists and those who deal with aesthetics of response, between the deconstructionists and the neonaturalists—any one of these theorists can predictably respond to a given text regardless of his individual generosity, meanness, or more or less felicitous writing style. No matter how unbiased reviewing theorists may seek to be, they discover in the text under review the flaws, gaps, ruptures, contradictions that their own theory sets out to expose. Books that support one's view are obviously much easier to praise than those that question or attack it.

The theorists known as the neo-Aristotelians (also called the "Chicago Critics") had a systematic way of reviewing theoretical books based on their premise that various literary criticisms and theories were distinct and more or less incommensurable "frameworks" or "languages." The approach to any theoretical language, therefore, was a matter "of assumed principle, definition and method." R. S. Crane declared that these "are not likely to show themselves, save indirectly, on the surface of a critic's discourse, and hence not likely, even in controversy, to force themselves on his attention. They pertain rather to what he thinks *with* than to what he thinks *about*—to the implicit structure and rationale of his argument as a whole than to the explicit doctrines he is attempting to state."[8]

Such a procedure makes reviewing systematic and comprehensible, but it also gives a false uniformity to the reviewing and writing process. It misconceives the way writing of theory takes place, and it neglects the interconnections among various types of "frameworks" or "languages." It creates systematic and coherent frameworks that belie what the authors are actually doing. In this procedure the reviewer conceals, though not consciously, the social and political interests which govern him and which a Marxist like Eagleton makes primary. But as feminist critics have argued, a disregard for recognizing or acknowledging one's own preferences makes prejudices seemingly nonexistent. By systematizing the unsystematic, this procedure reduces the complexity and often eliminates the insights a book possesses.

This kind of reviewing was an attempt to bring a "framework" system to the study of literature, an attempt to give it an analytical rigor. It provided a pluralistic approach while disregarding how theorists reviewing other theorists were entangled with their own and society's values. Reviewing was never a neutral enterprise, and from its beginning it was tied to journals as "institutions."

Reviewing as a professional activity dates from the establishment of reviewing journals in the eighteenth century. John Gross noted in *The Rise and Fall of the Man of Letters* that "with the rise of the professional author came the rise of the professional critic." The extension of the publishing industry brought with it reviewing journals that helped publicize and thus increase distribution of books: "The first successful reviews, the *Monthly* and the *Critical*, were both established in the reign of George II, and by the end of the eighteenth century other competitors had taken the field. At their worst these periodicals were little more than thinly-disguised publishers' catalogues, at their best they carried competent, respectable, even original work."[9] But the professional author and the increase in the number of publications were not the only bases for the development of reviewing journals. John Clive has pointed out that the numerous eighteenth-century clubs and societies in Edinburgh provided the "essential fertile soil for cooperative literary projects such as the [*Edinburgh*] *Review*" founded in 1802. He remarked that the earlier reviews— *The Monthly Review* (from 1749), *The Critical Review* (from 1756), the *Analytical Review* (from 1788)—were primarily abstracts of "the latest works on politics, literature, science and art. The emphasis on abstracts lasted, in varying degrees, throughout the century."[10] It was the *Edinburgh Review* that became at the beginning of the nineteenth century the most successful reviewing journal available. Its reviewers were, of course, professional literary men.

IV. Reviewing and Valuing

At present, reviewers and authors of theoretical books are almost always members of academic institutions. This means that they are involved in departmental as well as professional reviews. Thus their reviews are not merely scholarly exercises but instances of power. They have impact on the academic and economic advancement of the author, but also of the reviewer as author. For this reason scholarly reviews in our times have become an occasion for publicity and scholarly exposure. Scholarly reviewers are, if they give thought to their task, confronted with moral dilemmas as a result of the institutionalization of authors since reviews are among the determinants of advancement. First books, especially, constitute a moral problem for the reviewer. This may result in an eminent scholar like W. J. Bate reviewing and praising the book of his student or it may result in a senior reviewer refusing to review the book of a young scholar if he finds that he disapproves of some of the arguments in it. It is one thing to quarrel with the arguments of Stanley Fish or M. H. Abrams or Jacques Derrida; quite another to quarrel with the book of an unknown assistant professor.

It may seem that matters of academic appointment or economic advancement are irrelevant in reviewing books and that the examples I have given of reviewing or not reviewing are relatively infrequent. It may even be claimed that in loosening the meanings of "review" and "reviewing," I have muddled what is a very specific activity. To these objections I would reply that "reviewing" is an activity that in our time has become intimately connected with authority and power in contrast to early forms of reviewing as abstracts and summaries. Moreover, reviewing for us has connected the members of the academy with the production of reviews and the writing of books—and these are academic and economic interrelations. But I would make a further point, namely, that theoretical texts are especially concerned with moral issues. No matter whether a literary theory involves the nature of reading or the deconstruction of language, the theorist offers it as a value that will enhance the lives of those who pursue it. If a theorist defends "slow reading," he does so because it enhances the reader's appreciation and understanding.[11] And such activities are valuable because they make individuals more adequate members of society. If a scholar proposes a genre theory, he may do so because he wishes to explore generic change and, through this, the functions of change in society.

In the writing of a review, the reviewer acts as adviser to readers (and sometimes) to the author. But the basis of his description, analysis, and judgment is some larger view of the aim of the text. Whether the book deals with the rise or nature of the novel, the function of rhetoric, the nature of meaning or imagination, the reviewer assesses it in terms of its contribution to a field. But a literary field is worked by students, scholars, and teachers and they judge contributions by their "value." In this sense a reviewer envisages certain values for his field, and his review is governed by his explicit or implicit claims for literary study. And this applies as well to deconstructionists who find the languages of reviewers as well as those of texts self-contradictory. For even though it may appear pointless to write what is in itself unreliable, the very art of writing can be considered a moral gesture demonstrating the need to be skeptical of such gestures.

Given the varied views of reviewers, it may be asked how far a reader can trust a reviewer. What reliance can a reader place in a reviewer's comments, descriptions, evaluations? If reviews are governed by the premises of a reviewer, if his decisions are moral because they are related to his concern for the fate of society or for the author's fate or for his own, how can the reviewer offer his audience a reliable description and judgment of a text?

The trust that a reader gives to a reviewer should, under present reviewing conditions, be withheld. Until the reader has made an effort to read the book and assess the remarks of the reviewer, such remarks are untested and uncontested. It may, however, be useful to know whether a review can be tested or examined; whether mediated language can be weighed, or prejudices discounted, or hidden assumptions exposed. Since the mediated language introduces distortions, can the nature of the distortions be gauged by the reviewer's recognition of the difference between his language and the author's? Efforts toward this have been made by including extended quotations from the text, by sifting the vocabulary under review. Theorists employ terms like *text, absence, presence, transaction, other, discourse,* etc. in special ways. The reviewer who seeks to redefine these to convey the author's private use of a theoretical language is, at the very least, not resisting the special vocabulary an author introduces. He makes an effort to distinguish between an author's language and his own. This does not eliminate mediated language, but it makes the review reader conscious of it.

The reviewer brings to his task his own theoretical commitments and he reads the book under review against these. If he believes that theoretical books are written within language frameworks, he will seek to present the framework in detail, laying out the principles, definitions, methods. But if he believes that a work is composed of discursive formations, he will seek to explicate the epistemological assumptions of these formations. The reviewer, in describing these hypotheses, often notes that they can be completely circular and thus self-confirming. M. H. Abrams puts it this way: "The reason that all these modes of Newreading work is that each practitioner brings to the language of a text a ruling hypothesis about the kind of things it must necessarily mean or fail to mean, then deploys tactics that provide ample degrees of interpretive freedom to ensure that the hypothesis applies, by ruling out in advance any possible recourse that might serve to disconfirm it."[12]

But confirmation or disconfirmation is not the issue. Theoretical constructs are not inherent in language or literature; theorists formulate them for varied purposes. Such constructs are demonstrated in practice; they provide explanations for the pertinent subject matter. A reviewer, therefore, finds himself examining the specific examples offered or he offers his own in order to examine the construct. But no theory can or should be disengaged from explanations offered by other theorists; rather, any theory leads back to the question, what aims are served by its explanation or interpretation? The reviewer may thus find himself involved in questions about interpretive communities or the nature and aims of educational institutions, or the relation of art to morals.

It is easy to see how tempting for the theoretical reviewer is the pluralistic approach—the acceptance of different theories each of which seeks to be, even though it seldom is, consistent and coherent in its own terms. And tempting, too, is the assumption that although different approaches are acceptable, one's own is preferable to that of others. These are the lines reviewers take, along with the search for chinks in the system—for contradictions, inconsistencies, incoherence. But none of these seem to me to question the reasons for the initiation of a theory or the changes it makes in previous theories. A reviewer of a theoretical book ought to ask where, in the present realm of theoretical thinking, does the text belong? The problems it deals with are self-evidently a reviewer's task to consider, but why the selection of these problems and to what purpose? Why propose a generic theory, or a theory of "literature" in contrast to "nonliterature"? Why a theory of deconstruction or of capitalist production?

Why in studying Bunyan's *Grace Abounding* is it useful or perhaps necessary to raise the generic question of what constitutes an autobiography? Why is it necessary or even desirable to posit a theory of metaphor or allegory in order to discuss the specific uses of these in *The Waste Land*? What educational and social purposes are served by such theoretical works as Frye's *Anatomy of Criticism*, Wellek and Warren's *Theory of Literature*, Derrida's *Of Grammatology*? A reviewer of a theory book can easily avoid such questions by analyzing the theory itself, but the aims of a theory no less than the aims of poetry ought not to be ignored. A theoretical reviewer needs to see his task in terms of the discipline of letters and literature, in terms of the role it plays in the drama of society.

Psychoanalytic theories may deal with the transaction between the reviewer's self and that of the author in the text; they explore how the language of the self shapes and is shaped by the language of the text. But the larger social aim is the rehumanizing of the individual and thus the rehumanizing of society. Feminist critics who rely on psychoanalysis as the basis for gender criticism are equally concerned with identifying the feminist self in the reading transaction. My point is that any theory—whether it be deconstructive, structural, rhetorical, etc.—is concerned with the function of texts in the making of society.

It is apparent that a reviewer, in analyzing the societal aims of a theory, may find himself having to explain a theory that deals with an aspect of language such as metaphor rather than with poetic language in general, with the Gothic novel rather than with the novel. Theories are more or less comprehensive, and those of Northrop Frye or Kenneth Burke or R. S. Crane or Jacques Derrida, who seek to theorize about "literature" or all writing, are more comprehensive than Paul Ricoeur's in *The Rule of Metaphor*. It is the task of the reviewer to point out the range of theory, and in doing so, to indicate which theories the author is opposing and which he is supplementing by variations, or revising by omissions or alterations.

V. Theoretical Reviewing as Historical Inquiry

This implies that any "literary" theory is a historical text; it is composed to deal with, to explain, to initiate, to oppose certain kinds of writing of a certain place and time—no matter whether the place is the Western world or the time two thousand years. A theory is to be understood in terms of the kinds of texts to which it refers, and to other texts—theoretical and nontheoretical—with which it is contemporaneous. A theory is itself a kind of writing and it belongs with them as part of a historical period or movement or school.

Confirmation or disconfirmation of a theory is not often possible, even though specific references may be disconfirmed. But even if it were possible it would not explain why such a theory should be proposed at this particular time. The reviewer who sees himself as a historical being will wish to know what elements or features or aspects of past theories are being continued. He will see his review as a group of statements relating the book under review to others in the past, carrying on some of the views of literature, of unity, of intention, of value. This he does by attending to redefined terms, to the initiation of new ones, to the problems neglected or confronted, to the continuities and changes based on previous theories, to discourse elements and their interrelations with other kinds of writing.

The most obvious historical procedure is for the reviewer to note the changes that take place with the author's own theoretical premises. Thus Paul de Man's early essay "Symbolic Landscape in Wordsworth and Yeats" (1963) was an example of New Critical analysis with its search for tension, complexity, and an underlying unity and wholeness, a belief that there is a "key" to interpretation of the poem. [13] The close reading is not abandoned with its analysis of individual terms and images. But the concept of the whole is and with it the assumption of the special power of poetic imagery. The reviewer of *Blindness and Insight* or *Allegories of Reading* would have to explain how a shift in the conception of poetic language and unity undermined the previous views that sought the independence of the student reader as one of its goals.

The author who writes self-consciously of the changes in his own writing—as Paul de Man, Jerome McGann, and Elaine Showalter do—provides the reviewer with an autobiographical awareness of historical change. But such awareness places the reviewer in a position to describe an author's revision and to evaluate an author's sense of self. There is no reason to assume that an author's judgment reflects anything more than his own limitations—but these become apparent to reviewers through his particular form of self-consciousness.

Consider the recent recantation of Jerome McGann in *The Romantic Ideology* (1983): "I should like to conclude with an illustrative case from Byron, partly because I have been to some extent responsible for perpetuating certain misconceptions about his work, and partly because Byron's late achievements can sometimes appear to have transcended his own Romantic illusions. The 'poetic development' of Byron which I argued in *Fiery Dust* now seems to me a most misleading critical formulation." What the reviewer faces here is the claim that Byron's late poetry remains a romantic delusion and that it does not avoid the inadequate self-assessment of the romantics. Byron's art can make readers miss "the ideas and ideologies which lead him into a disclosure of his world's contradictions by tempting him to believe that they can be transcended in imaginative thought. . . . In the end Byron's poetry discovers . . . that there is no place of refuge, not in desire, not in the mind, not in imagination."[14]

The reviewer who finds McGann's earlier book on Byron,

Fiery Dust, a more adequate interpretation than his later, will present the reasons for such disagreement. Is the quality of a poem determined by its awareness of its contradictions? This would seem a peculiar argument to offer since the very qualities that Byron is aware of would not be those that are located by the theorist. The very concept of concealed contradiction is imposed by the theorist, and there is no reason for assuming that the poet in making such contradictions evident becomes a better artist. McGann does not deny the value of the English stanzas of *Don Juan*, but it is not at all clear in what this value consists since, for him, the stanzas illustrate the inadequacy of thought characteristic of all romantic poetry.

The reviewer who sees himself as a historical inquirer realizes the tentative role he performs in our time. His role as middleman between author and reader has become ambiguous; his obligation as narrator is neither neutral nor objective. He often competes as author with the author of the book he is reviewing. His own views of theory are written into the review he writes—intentionally or unintentionally. His guidance is suspect since it is often governed by motives that are concealed from the reader. In a time of competing and burgeoning theories, the historical reviewer can, at best, disclose his own preferences and prejudices. He becomes, therefore, not a reliable guide but an advocate of a theoretical position. Reviewing is becoming in our time an analogue to literary theory; it becomes an independent genre often discussing the reviewer's interests rather than those of the text under review.

Can reviewing become a reliable guide? It can but only if the reviewing procedure is reconceived. If reviews were published with answers by the author, the reader would be in a position to examine contrary arguments. Reviews of this kind would be dialogues between authors and reader-reviewers. Reviews *could* then be part of an ongoing inquiry into the theoretical problems raised; such dialogues would deal with specific issues that would engage both participants in noting agreements and disagreements. Such a procedure would present author and reviewer together and the reader would thus have before him a sample of the oppositional views and the styles in which they are com-posed. Scholarly journals often publish forums or letters in which replies to reviews are made months after the reviews have been published. Such procedures make performances out of such interchanges; they have little to do with clarifying issues.

Publishing an author's response together with a review would not alter the institutional pressures exerted on reviewers, but it would modify the search for originality and the emphasis on theoretical differences. It would help to clarify for the reader the arguments that are offered, and it would make possible a concep-tion of reviewing as a cooperative inquiring. And it might, just might, create a sense of common enterprise in the study of theory that is clearly absent today.

The solution is not meant as a panacea or as an effort to provide some single unified theory with which all theorists will agree. Reviewers will remain as varied as before. But they will at least realize that they are addressing the author and are subject to his reply. This may make them less untrustworthy and more re-sponsible as interpreters and judges. But what if, in this dialogue, reviewer and author agree? Here, surely, review readers have grounds for suspicion. Perhaps, then, we can turn to the book itself.

Notes

1. Eagleton, *Literary Theory* (Minneapolis: Univ. of Minnesota Press, 1983), p. 204.
2. De Man, *The Rhetoric of Romanticism* (New York: Columbia Univ. Press, 1984), p. viii.
3. Eagleton, p. 204.
4. Wellek and Warren, *Theory of Literature* (New York: Harcourt, Brace, 1949), pp. 30–31.
5. Eric Bentley, ed., "A Reply to F. R. Leavis," *The Importance of Scrutiny* (New York: Grove, 1948), p. 32.
6. Krieger, *Theory of Criticism* (Baltimore: Johns Hopkins Univ. Press, 1976), p. 7.
7. Scholes, *Textual Power* (New Haven: Yale Univ. Press, 1985), p. 19.
8. Crane, *The Languages of Criticism and the Structure of Poetry* (Toronto: Univ. of Toronto Press, 1953), p. 13.
9. Gross, *The Rise and Fall of the Man of Letters* (New York: Collier Books, 1970), p. 1.

10. Clive, *Scotch Reviewers: The Edinburgh Review, 1802–1815* (London: Faber and Faber, 1957), pp. 21, 31.

11. Reuben A. Brower, "Reading in Slow Motion," *In Defense of Reading*, ed. Brower and Richard Poirier (New York: Dutton, 1963), pp. 19–20.

12. "Literary Criticism in America," Occasional Papers of the Council of Scholars, no. 2, *Theories of Criticism*, by M. H. Abrams and James Ackerman (Washington, D.C.: Library of Congress, 1984), p. 29.

13. Brower, pp. 22–37.

14. McGann, *Romantic Ideology* (Chicago: Univ. of Chicago Press, 1983), pp. 138, 145.

Derek Pearsall

Reviewing Literary History (Medieval)

The practice of book reviewing is part of the book trade. Publishers believe that it is commercially advantageous to supply free copies of new books to journals of good repute, or, sometimes, simply to journals that ask for them. They are led to understand, in that innocent and gullible way publishers have, that the sales of their books will be enhanced by having them noticed or reviewed, and they adjust the budget for the book to allow for the cost of such publicity. The publisher's action constitutes, in this market, the demand. The journal, whether operating on a commercial or scholarly basis, acts as the entrepreneur in the transaction, the reviews themselves being supplied by scholars, experts, hacks, or "reviewers" (these are people who seem to do nothing else). The incentives they have to act in this manner are various. One incentive may be greed, whether for the small sums of money that certain journals make available for reviews, or for the acquisition of a free copy of the book. It is not unknown for those scholars who have an eye to profit to volunteer to review books of a particularly expensive nature, while of course professional reviewers would expect to offload most of their mangled carcases onto the second-hand stalls.

Discounting greed, for possession or profit, one has to recognize that there are various other kinds of vicious impulse that reviewing may serve: anger, for instance, at the book or its author or at the world in general, where the adoption of the ostensibly even-handed and judicious role of the reviewer may be the means through which he uses it, like Chaucer's Pardoner, "to spit out his venom under hue of holiness"; or mere vanity, amongst those who are tickled by the invitation to pontificate, and who have no greater desire or happiness than to see themselves in print. Stronger still as an impelling motive in the reviewers of our day is the calculation of professional advantage, which contributes to that turning upside down of the market whereby the review becomes the marketable commodity and the book the occasion of sale. A review can be given a modest place in its author's curriculum vitae, and so it becomes an item in the food chain which makes for academic survival. Its part in the world of academic "getting-on" is ironically surveyed by Spearing: "We all know . . . that academics need to publish articles and books in order to gain appointment, tenure, and promotion; that articles and books merely repeating what has been said before do not usually get published; and that it is therefore necessary to fabricate new interpretations, however absurd. The publication of books surveying these interpretations is yet another manifestation of the same deplorable process; and so, in its small way, is the publication of reviews of these books."[1] How much further, one may think, from any center of living experience is the activity of contributing an essay to a book *about* reviews?

But enough of such dispiriting contemplation. There must be something else that explains the willingness of an academic scholar to take on the burden of reading a not very good book, assigning it its place in near oblivion, and bearing the consequence of doing unwanted justice; and it cannot be mere stupidity. One must assume that an important incentive for the reviewer is the belief in the good of his subject and in the ability of reviewing to serve that good. This assumption I shall attempt to hold to through the rest of this essay.

It must be said that the prejudice against or neglect of book reviewing among academics, of which James O. Hoge and James L. W. West III have spoken, is well established and to some extent well justified.[2] The power of the reviewer to wound without being in danger of receiving hurt, to deliver accolades or thunderbolts at a whim, can make him a nasty customer, a hit-and-run driver of the academic highways. There is also such a grotesque inequity in the burden borne by the author in the production of a book, and the corresponding burden borne by the reviewer in reviewing it, that natural justice cries out for the latter's power to be curbed. Ignorance, idleness, and prejudice are as common amongst writers of books as amongst the reviewers of them, but the former are at least obliged to come clean, and at length: the reviewer, on the other hand, can avoid talking about the areas where he is incompetent whilst selecting the more obviously hittable targets. The author makes some kind of commitment to his subject, spends some months or years of his life on the book, offers himself up to criticism, where the reviewer spends whatever is left of a couple of days on his task, at the same time seeing himself as the agent of some large public judgment against which there is no appeal. The author, however he may fume at injustice and the spurning of merit, is well advised to remain silent in the face of an ignorant or unfair review, since there is nothing that is thought more pathetic than an author's protest against a review. The public's view of him is as full of sympathy as for the lion tamer who gets his head bitten off by the lion, and their view is entirely understandable given that, amongst the various respectable reasons for reading reviews—finding out whether a book is worth buying, making sure that a book is not worth buying, acquiring conversation fodder—one important reason is always the prospective delight in a massacre, or in the swathes that may be cut through the groves of professional reputation. A "swingeing" or "devastating" review (the language of aggression is often very much in evidence) is much more fun to read than a long book, and takes a lot less time.

A good many reviewers of the edition of the B-Version of *Piers Plowman* by George Kane and E. Talbot Donaldson were somewhat incensed by a remark made by the editors at the end of their introduction: "We offer our text, then, as a restored B version of *Piers Plowman*. . . . The apparatus supporting that text contains all material evidence. . . . How we have interpreted that evidence . . . has been laid wholly open to scrutiny in the preceding pages of this Introduction. Whether we have carried out our task efficiently must be assessed by reenacting it."[3] It looked like an injunction against reviewers, and seemed not only improper but actually wrong, since it is in the nature of an edition that many of its individual judgments will be open to individual and even independent scrutiny, particularly so with an edition that proclaims the death of recension and the status of every substantive textual variant as a potential editorial crux to be dealt with to some extent in its own terms. Some reviewers took issue, understandably, with what they saw as a rather highhanded and magisterial prohibition; there were few, however, who did not come to realize that there was some truth in the editors' assumption of superiority, and who did not find, for instance, that their own criticisms, as they got further into the edition, had been anticipated and, to some extent at least, answered. It is a book that, by the quality of its scholarship rather than by its own admonitions, humbles the reviewer, and it is perhaps no accident that reviews of the Kane-Donaldson B-text were, by and large, notable for their length, their effort to match the scholarship of the edition, and the care and time that had obviously been expended on them.

The book I have chosen to illustrate this point is an edition of a text, and though the particular aspect of book reviewing I have agreed to talk about is the reviewing of books on "literary history" (a genre I interpret fairly broadly in my examination of the specifically medieval field—the only one I know anything about), it is nevertheless on this point that I should like, in the first instance, to insist: the reviewer should see himself, initially, as the servant of the book, should be open to receive it on its own terms, and should strive to retain this posture of respectful humility for as long as a book seems to deserve it. There are many other temptations, and some of them have been described above, but the honest reviewer must begin with the belief that he is in the presence of a masterpiece and with the recognition that his own role is that of acolyte. The worst kind of review, both uninformative and misleading, is that in which the reviewer proceeds immediately to the grinding of his own ax, oblivious of doubt and still more so of any notion that the benefit might be given to it.

This openmindedness and respect characterize the state of mind in which the reviewer begins his reading, and are the only means through which some measure of objectivity can be achieved. By the time he has completed his reading, of course, and taken his notes for his review, he may be in a position to recognize that his trust was misplaced and, with his goodwill exhausted and with some exasperation at the time wasted on an unprofitable labor, he may take out his hatchet. He may think at this point that it would have been better to have declined the invitation to review the book, and certainly anyone who *knows* that he is going to dislike a book has an obligation to decline such an invitation. But our reviewer, if he has approached his task in the right spirit, and has been brought to his ill opinion by good and secure routes, has now a duty to complete his task. There are, however, two things he must do before he embarks on evaluation, namely, précis and contextualization, not necessarily in that order.

From any point of view, and with regard to any use to which a review may be put, the indispensable element in it is an indication of the contents of the book. The normal relationship of the reviewer to the reader of the review is that of a person who has read the book to a person who has not, and whatever else the reviewer does will be useless without an honest and accurate account of the book's contents. It is the most difficult thing to do well: opinions are ten-a-penny and the pungent phrase a mere gift, but précis is one of the most strenuous and demanding of all intellectual activities. The publisher's blurb is at this point to be avoided at all costs: if it was written by the publisher's editor, it will be vapid and inaccurate; if it was written by the author, it will have been done in that state of exhaustion and nervous prostration which follows on delivery, and will contain reference only to what he might have done, or thinks he has done, or even to what he thinks may satisfy the publisher's importunacies. Strict précis, chapter by chapter, is sometimes too tedious a process, and may allow too much to the author's specialized decisions in the organization of his material. The most proper way may be the hard way, that is, the complete digestion of the book's argument and the reproduction of that argument, accurately proportioned, in succinct terms. Particular kinds of books set particular kinds of difficulty: works of literary history which are as much descriptive as evaluative, such as the books by Rosemary Woolf on the medieval English religious lyric and on the medieval English drama, cannot be summarised.[4] In such a case the main lines of approach have to be isolated, and may have to be unwoven from the thick texture of description. A work of pure literary history is still more difficult to review, unless the book is done from some specific point of view (such as a Marxist history of Arthurian literature),[5] and reviewers of my own book on *Old English and Middle English Poetry* found themselves mostly bemused as to what might be said in the way of précis, as well as bewildered, in a kindly way, as to why such a book should have been written.[6] Worst of all is the festchrift, or book of essays by several hands, where the impossibility of saying something about everything, the sense of duty shirked in giving a mere list of contents (which would in fact probably be the most useful thing to do in the circumstances), leads to all kinds of fudging.

Whatever the difficulties, a good summary of the book under review is essential, and may contribute to the permanent usefulness of the review. An offprint or illegally obtained photocopy of the review can be tucked away in one's copy of the book and will provide a handy reminder of its contents. I have a copy of Friedman's review of Burrow's *Ricardian Poetry* that I use in this way,[7] though it must be said that the review exemplifies one of the vices of the genre as well as one of its important virtues: Friedman spends nearly a page chastising Burrow for a passing remark about medieval art, chiefly because Friedman finds that he knows a good deal more about this subject than his author, not because it is essential to the evaluation of his book.

Accurate and succinct summary, then, is important in a review, and is made particularly useful if it contains brief and well-chosen quotation. Almost equally important is the provision of that context of understanding in which a book is to be placed. Here the reviewer's own depth of knowledge in the subject is tested, his experience in this case rather than simply his intellect.

Ideally, he should have read the other books published by the author under review as well as a respectable proportion of the books that the author has read, and he should be able in a few sentences to "tell the story so far"—to give the essential historical background to the subject, the key books, the current movements and trends, so that the book under review will be seen to take its place in the historical continuum. Nothing is more difficult than to do this objectively and briefly. The author himself may of course be very conscious of the place of his book in the historical continuum, and he should be, but something larger and more objective is demanded of the reviewer. He has a better chance of achieving this wider and more detached overview if he is reviewing a number of related books at the same time, in a relatively long piece. An excellent example of this type of "review article" is provided by Lee Patterson in an account of books on Chaucer by Donald Howard, Robert Burlin, Alfred David, and John Gardner,[8] and of course the provision of opportunities for this kind of omnibus review has become a regular practice of the journal *Review*.

When these two stages are completed—and a well-shaped review can often combine the activities of contextualization and précis in quite a successful way—the reviewer may be permitted to express his considered evaluation of the book, though there will be few who by now have not given some hint of their opinion. Some books may be so good that there is nothing to give but unstinted praise—a rather embarrassing situation for the reviewer to find himself in, since he may feel that his occupation's gone—but in nearly all cases evaluation will be hinged on a "but": general commendation will be followed by specific adverse criticisms or, more commonly, specific commendations by reservations about the whole. Some reviewers find it almost impossible to avoid this "sic et non" structure, and tend to construct every sentence in the form of an antithesis. This is what is often construed as well-balanced and objective judgment, though in reality it is often no more than a nervous reflex to the demands of the genre, and a way of hedging. It may lead to a sort of coziness, an invitation to mutual back scratching in which today's reviewer knows he may be tomorrow's reviewed. Authors will claim to be variously affected by reviews of their books, and certainly some are more neurotic than others, but it is rare to come across one who is unaffected or who would fail to read a review of one of his books that he came across from beginning to end, even if he did not seek it out, with considerable interest.

Some kinds of evaluation, readily entered into in a review, are unfair. The collecting of factual errors, and the stringing together of such errors in bunches, is usually unfair. No book can be altogether free of such errors, and a hawkish reviewer, in gathering half-a-dozen howlers, may well have seized on almost everything in the book that is impermissible and given a false impression of its reliability as a whole. An appropriate way of dealing with such errors, in books that are thought to be worth the trouble, and where the author and a possible second edition may be improved, is to set them as a kind of appendix to the main review. A number of journals, such as the *Modern Language Review*, allow occasionally for this to be done in smaller type. Typographical errors can be dealt with in the same way: the reviewer's ability to note misspellings, and the Olympian scorn that he will consider appropriate to be provoked in him by them, has not much to do with his responsibilities as a reviewer. A particular obloquy might properly be claimed to attach to errors in quoted material, especially quotations from the literary texts that the author purports to be examining. A review by Edward Wilson of David L. Jeffrey's book on *The Early English Lyric and Franciscan Spirituality* did little more than cite a whole series of such errors, some of which produced mere gibberish in the quoted text, and then abandon the book as hopeless: "This is a thoroughly shoddy piece of work. When the primary sources are so inaccurately presented and so imperfectly understood this reviewer sees no profit in discussing the speculations which Mr. Jeffrey has based upon them."[9] This is probably fair, if harsh.

In all this, one has to recognize that the reviewer can always produce the impression he wants by selection of the evidence, or at least by a presentation of the evidence out of context. His investment in his work as a reviewer, as was pointed out earlier, is strictly limited, indeed, so little as to encourage irresponsibility, and there is nothing easier than to bring together stylistic infelicities, or even mere repetitions, in such a way as to suggest that a book is more or less illiterate. The reviewer should restrain his enthusiasm here, or at least restrain his irritable inclination to get into his review everything he has troubled to make a note of. Such carping is of infinitesimal significance beside the responsibility he should always be aware of to relate whatever he says about the book he is reviewing to the historical tradition of criticism and to the canons of criticism and taste that he himself endorses. At best, it ought to be possible to collect the work of an individual reviewer and to trace in it, along with the proper due of respect to the argument and opinions of the book under review, a consistency of viewpoint that gives coherence to the whole body of writing.

If the structure of a review and the standards it adopts for evaluation can be seen as a matter of the observance of good models and practice, style, finally, is altogether more a matter of individual taste. Yet it may have more influence and more persuasive power than anything else. A classic instance, and one worth rereading in its entirety, is the review by Derek Brewer of *Fruyt and Chaf* by Huppé and Robertson. This review does all the right things, is informative, objective, based on clear and consistent critical principles, and yet it is in the end the genially dismissive manner of the review that most fully sets the book in its place. Brewer concludes his review thus: "The final paradox is that this book must therefore be regarded as a work, not of criticism or scholarship, but of literature in its own right; a series of unfalsifiable fantasies of great interest, growing out of the contemplation of Chaucer's poetry by two learned and amiable, if intellectually somewhat eccentric scholars. It is most attractive and stimulating; enthusiastic, full of curious information, and remarkably ingenious. Dangerous for young students who may confuse its genre, mature scholars should enjoy it."[10] No book was ever consigned to the scrapheap with such urbane goodwill. As Horace Walpole said of the Mausoleum at Castle Howard, it would be almost worth being buried if one could be sure of being buried like that.

Notes

1. A. C. Spearing, in a review of Alice R. Kaminsky, *Chaucer's Troilus and Criseyde and the Critics* (Athens: Ohio Univ. Press, 1980), in *Review of English Studies*, n.s., 34 (1983):206.
2. Hoge and West, "Academic Book Reviewing: Some Problems and Suggestions," *Scholarly Publishing* 11 (1979):35–41.
3. *Piers Plowman: The B-Version*, ed. George Kane and E. Talbot Donaldson (London: Athlone Press, 1975), p. 220.
4. Woolf, *The English Religious Lyric in the Middle Ages* (Oxford: Clarendon Press, 1968); *The English Mystery Plays* (London: Routledge and Kegan Paul, 1972).
5. For example, Stephen Knight, *Arthurian Literature and Society* (London: Macmillan, 1983).
6. E.g., Anne Hudson, in a review of Derek Pearsall, *Old English and Middle English Poetry* (London: Routledge and Kegan Paul, 1977), in *Review of English Studies*, n.s., 29 (1978):191–93.
7. A review by John Block Friedman of J. A. Burrow, *Ricardian Poetry: Chaucer, Gower, Langland and the Gawain Poet* (London: Routledge and Kegan Paul, 1971), in *Journal of English and Germanic Philology* 73 (1974): 241–44.
8. Lee W. Patterson, "Writing about Writing: The Case of Chaucer," *University of Toronto Quarterly* 48 (1978–79):172–91.
9. Wilson, in a review of Jeffrey, *The Early English Lyric and Franciscan Spirituality* (Lincoln: Univ. of Nebraska Press, 1975), in *Review of English Studies*, n.s., 28 (1977):321.
10. Derek S. Brewer, in a review of Bernard F. Huppé and D. W. Robertson, Jr., *Fruyt and Chaf: Studies in Chaucer's Allegories* (Princeton: Princeton Univ. Press, 1963), in *Review of English Studies*, n.s., 16 (1965):305.

Stanley Weintraub

Reviewing Literary Biography: Apprehending the *Daimon*

"Art," says Umberto Eco, "is an escape from personal emotion." Not so the art of biography, despite its nonfiction form. Regardless of the extent and depth of the materials upon which a biography is based, biographers must intervene among them, make their choices, develop interpretations, conceive strategies for transforming the amorphous mass into a life. In the process, something of the personality of the biographer intrudes itself into the biography, and that quality becomes the crucial element in the book for the critic to apprehend. In effect it is the lens through which the documentation of the life has been viewed: the critic must measure the refraction.

Bernard Shaw was wrong, then, when as a young man he wrote of Henry Raeburn, in reviewing a biography, that it was Raeburn's "happiness to leave no history except a catalog of his works." The Scottish painter had nevertheless failed to fend off a biography—a fact that suggested as much about the indefatigable biographer as about his subject.

Faced with the inevitability of his own biography, present or posthumous, many a writer has wished to leave no history but his own works, and has even enjoined his heirs not to publish, or to permit publication, of his letters or facilitate in any way the production of a biography. Doing so has only demonstrated blindness to Oscar Wilde's insight that his art lay more in his life than in his works. Since biographers have long intuited that paradox, no such injunction from the grave kept Orwell or Auden or Maugham or Hemingway from becoming subjects for lives, or from having their surviving letters collected and edited.

Hoarding of manuscript rights by Orwell's widow failed to hold off the biographers, for she could not prevent a two-volume life from being constructed entirely out of public-domain materials and frugal application of the fair-use doctrine to copyright publications. Even the stonewalling about an authorized biography on the part of T. S. Eliot's fiercely protective widow, who has carefully restricted access to unpublished letters, and has refused permission to publish much copyright material, has done little to stem a flood of memoirs, biographies—even a biographical play at the Royal Court Theatre and a television documentary on BBC 2—about her curious husband. As for the living writer who has left his biographical trail everywhere before becoming alert to the likelihood of a literary biography, no pyromaniac descent upon the papers in his own physical possession can prevent the dreaded books from appearing. All it can do is impoverish their texture by plucking a dimension or two from the portrait. Further, obscuring motive or impulse only furnishes opportunities for speculation possibly more damaging than the truth. James Boswell once fantasized, "I had lately a thought that appeared new to me: that by burning all my journal and all my written traces of former life, I should be like a new being. . . . Were I just now to go and take up house in any country town in England, it would be just a different existence." The inhibitions of ego were too much. The journals survived and added dimensions to what we know of his life that might otherwise have been missing, but had his dream of obliterating the records been realized, we would have had a biography anyway— a different one in details and nuances. For he could not have done away with records in other locations, memories in other heads, letters in other hands.

Literary biographies will happen, just as novels or poems will happen. The difference in genres lies in the critical tools we must bring to their evaluation and their utilization. Oscar Wilde was not merely joking when he wrote, "To know the vintage and quality of a wine one need not drink the whole cask. It must be perfectly easy in half an hour to say whether a book is worth anything or worth nothing. Ten minutes are really sufficient, if one has the instinct for form." But the books Wilde was talking about were poems and plays and novels. A work of fact—recording, digesting, selecting and analyzing facts—can be important, and even crucial, despite its style, in the face of its disorganization, notwithstanding its aesthetic inadequacies. Although in a literary biography one yearns for literary elegance worthy of its subject, without style it can still survive and even become an essential tool of further scholarship. In biography there is no last word even if there is no new information. As our fashions in people change, we grind fresh lenses with which to see them anew.

At their own risk, critics accept on faith the integrity or the scholarship of the biographer. A biography may be fiction masquerading as life, as with Wolfgang Hildesheimer's *Marbot: A Biography* (1983), a novel about an invented Sir Andrew Marbot, allegedly a friend of Wordsworth and Coleridge, by the author of a legitimate life of Mozart. Not a word of the jacket copy suggests the jeu d'esprit, and some librarians may have mis-shelved it. It even reads "straight" and is thoroughly convincing. Then there are the intended frauds, such as Clifford Irving's notorious *Howard Hughes*, purportedly based on Hughes's taped words, which cost Irving a jail term, and Antoni Gronowicz's life of Pope John Paul II, *God's Broker* (1984), allegedly based upon two hundred hours of conversation with the Pontiff, with whom the author was never alone. Even the jacket photograph showing Gronowicz shaking hands with John Paul II was cropped to suggest a private meeting.

Since publishers do not routinely check biographies for accuracy, the critic is often on his own. Even things we think are established truths may not be so, as with Sir Philip Sidney's battlefield offer of his water bottle to another dying soldier, or Sir Walter Raleigh's throwing down his cloak for Queen Elizabeth to walk on. To be skeptical without being cynical is a difficult reviewing posture to maintain. The reviewer is seldom suspicious, for example, of welcome new manuscript finds, yet in the age of the tape recorder the new documentation about contemporaries may even be electronic, and susceptible to electronic doctoring. Diaries, too, have been faked. Even distinguished historians were taken in by the *Stern* Adolf Hitler forgeries in 1983. But the most obvious form of biographical fakery—invented dialogue—should not escape any reader of biography. Any undocumented conversation must be considered fraudulent. Further, allegedly documented dialogue that sounds more like the written word than the spoken one may be a device to subvert words in copyright (and legally unavailable to the author) into the public domain. (Conversation is not under copyright.) Authenticity cannot always be established by the critic: he is at a distance from the documents. The appearance of authenticity, however, is easier to monitor. Something unnatural in context earns our suspicion.

One of the risks a literary biographer takes is competition with his subject. A literary figure worth writing about often has written very well indeed about an event or a person, and to reduce the narrative to paraphrase, after offering samples of the subject's prose, can be self-defeating. Even a subject on the margin of literature can be stylish or idiosyncratic, or attractively lucid, in ways that betray the lesser competence of the biographer. A critic's antennae will sometimes pick this up, as when Hermoine Lee reviewed Karen Monson's life of Alma Mahler, subtitled *Muse to Genius* (1984). Gustav Mahler had conducted *Tristan and Isolde* in the presence of his new love and his now jealous sister Justine, whose possessiveness had been nearly suffocating. The first act had been electrifying, Alma recalled. "The production was wonderful . . . but Mahler was tired. After the second act he lay on the sofa; his face was white, he could hardly pull himself together to conduct the third act. 'If only someone would take it off my hands,' he said. It was then Justine lost all that was left of my love for her. As we stood looking down on Mahler lying there, half asleep, she said under her breath: 'One thing delights me—I had his youth, you have him now [that] he's old.' "

Alma's biographer, working on the premise that the writer must say it in different words, turns the breathless recollection into clumsy dullness—all but the key quotation at the close. But the power of the quotation renders the new prose even more wretched: "At the first performance . . . Gustav was exhausted and during intermission he lay on the sofa in his private room and wished to give up and go away from all the problems of his position. Standing over him with Alma, Justi (Mahler's sister) commented, 'One thing delights me—I had his youth, you have him now he's old.' "

After some further examples, including some heavy-breathing ones, Hermione Lee concludes, "It's not just that Monson seems to be writing with two left feet. The 'legend' has been too much for her. Famous women with dramatic sex-lives do seem dangerous to their biographers—Jeffrey Meyers's *Katherine Mansfield*, Nancy Cardozo's *Maud Gonne*, and Joan Givner's *Katherine Anne Porter* are over-emotional examples of the genre." Regardless of biographical subject, however, the warning is clear. One need not write Jamesian prose in writing about Henry James, or Conradian prose in writing about Conrad; but in avoiding the competition, biographers must not flatten, or inflate, their own narratives. (Another problem in writing biographical prose is the temptation to anachronism. We must apply our contemporary insights and our new knowledge. But should a 1984 biographer of Boswell describe his subject's fits of laziness by observing that Boswell's "motor was idling"? A usage contemporary to Boswell might accomplish the same ends more effectively—and without historical dissonance.)

Narrative is narrative, whether in biography or the novel, and the critic has to apply many of the same tests to the one as the other. Both use dialogue, although the biographer must quote only the real thing. And both use such narrative devices as foreshadowing and flashback. For the biographer, invention lies only in technique and selection and style, not in the imaginative rendering of events and details. But the days are gone when a biographer had no choice but to set down solemnly the facts of a life from cradle to grave. In medias res serves the biographer as well as the poet. There is little reason, then, why an actual life (given adequate documentation) cannot be told as effectively as an imagined one, and possess as well the psychological impact of actuality. This person lived: our empathy can be all the more immediate and intense. If it is not, the fault is either in the art—or in the subject.

The biographer's choice of subject is his most crucial decision—although one can make anything of almost anyone, given imagination and documentation. Except in the case of established biographers, choice of subject may mean the difference between being widely and favorably reviewed, and not being noticed at all. That fact of literary life suggests why so many redundant and overlapping lives appear, and why publishers shy away from biographies of people whose names are not instantly recognizable, unless the name of the biographer is. The beguiled notion that a biographer must be an advocate can also complicate the matter of choice. A subject can be written about with gusto, yet not be a satisfactory human being, a role model for one's readers.

It is easy, however, to become an apologist for someone else's life. Why, after all, would one want to invest years of biographical research and writing on someone who was an obnoxious and bigoted windbag, whose hundred-plus books were largely junk, and who even smelled bad? A. N. Wilson, whose *Hilaire Belloc* (1984) was weighted with just such a problem, dealt with a curiously likeable but curmudgeonly person who usually backed the wrong causes and the wrong people with dogged persistence whatever the cost. As a husband and family man he was a failure; as a champion of Romanism he was a fraud (the Pope was a "greasy monsignore" and Jesus "a milksop"); as a literary giant he was bogus. Yet Wilson, having perceived all this, in concluding pages of peroration rushes nonetheless into what the military would call a "damage control" operation, as if special pleading for Belloc's flawed character and panoply of prejudices were necessary. In the process Belloc is labeled a literary "genius" and Wilson's earlier stylishness becomes more and more suspect. What he has failed to build into his biography is the total acceptance of the reality of what his subject is, or was. Explaining him and understanding his motives are crucial, rationalizing him and occasionally sympathizing with his behavior are counterproductive. The vital factor in the choice of subject is the interest of the personality or the achievement, which can capture us without quite making us captives. If the biographer had to begin with sympathy or admiration of a sort to inspire an implicit apologia, who would write about the world's monsters—a Hitler, a Stalin, a Nero, a Sade? It is a fact of biography, however, that writers about lives sometimes enter so fully into the life as to become tempted to offer justifications for the life rather than for the book.

The number of unsatisfactory personalities among literary people is legion, yet their lives can be handled with unindulgent scrupulousness, as in Anne Thwaite's *Edmund Gosse* (1984). As critic, biographer, and translator, Gosse was pathologically inaccurate; as a man on the social make he became a butterer-up of the aristocratic and well-placed; as a literary opportunist eager for more income than he needed he cast a blind eye at such sleazy and suspect friends as T. J. Wise the forger. Yet Anne Thwaite shows us simultaneously the other Edmund Gosse—the critic who encouraged young talents like W. B. Yeats and Aubrey Beardsley; who promoted (albeit in his bad translations) such notorious writers as Henrik Ibsen; who turned his miserable childhood at the hands of a fanatically religious father into a sensitive yet honest autobiographical novel, *Father and Son*, that remains one of the classics of the genre. In most ways a modest sort of monster, Gosse comes off as an endearing and amusing one—the intent matches that of Wilson's *Belloc*, but the unapologetic result is more successful.

Similarly, another energetic Victorian scholar-entrepreneur, W. J. Furnivall, promotor of the *New English Dictionary* (*O.E.D.*) and countless literary societies, might be portrayed via his many deficiencies, or have some of them overlooked or explained away. Again, like Gosse, he had no zeal for exactness, no guilt about taking on tasks for which he was unqualified, no qualms about misusing or misleading his friends. Unlike the prudent— even prudish and inhibited—Gosse, Furnivall was also an unabashed amorist, especially with working-class girls. Once, when he was nearly sixty, he even moved his new twenty-one-year-old mistress into the family house. (Mrs. Furnivall took their son and moved out.) A biographer might present Furnivall as colorful and even attractive—a Victorian monster of hypocrisy who felt no sense of it. By his own standards he was a man of rectitude; he neither smoked nor drank, encouraged scholars and critics who became fervent disciples, was tireless in opening windows into literature for the newly educated masses. By his own lights he was a good and generous man; by ours he was an outrageous Victorian of manic energy and very considerable achievement. William Benzie falters in his *Dr. F. J. Furnivall: Victorian Scholar Adventurer* (1983). The information is largely there, although the sexual side of the wicked old man is scanted, but Benzie strives so hard—as he explains in his preface—to avoid treating Furnivall as "merely another literary eccentric" in order to deal more fully with his achievement, that the work and the man remain unintegrated. Life escapes, not because a cover-up is intended, but because the author is afraid (for good reason!) that a powerful personality will overwhelm the productive side of his subject.

Some biographies born in indignation and in the urge to restore reputations work out better than one would have supposed when the biographer learns enough from the research effort to modify preliminary bias. Elinor Langer's *Josephine Herbst* (1984) began as a self-confessed radical feminist's rehabilitation of a maligned, and then forgotten, between-the-wars novelist and social activist. Then Langer discovered that her heroic earlier-generation feminist had not only lived a different kind of life than she had expected to find, but that her three major love affairs, all with people much younger than herself—two women and a man—showed a pattern of unfeminist abject dependence. As for her politics, Herbst's devotion to the Left, from domestic activism to risky foreign involvements, ended with the disillusion of Spain, although she did not break publicly with the Party because it would have meant repudiating her life. The rest was downhill. She kept on writing, although her income from it became marginal, and she maintained the new friendships which kept her going in a gypsylike existence when away from her primitive Pennsylvania farmhouse. It was less than a life of doctrinaire idealism, but whatever Langer's earlier intentions, she accommodates her biography to the evidence, in a rapport with her subject that she could not have anticipated. A desperate letter from Herbst to her husband, insincerely marked "DE-STROY," confessed, "You wrote my name in your own hand, not typed. I just licked every letter." Langer exposes the line, however demeaning to her heroine, and we understand Herbst better for it. Josie Herbst was too complicated for doctrinaire treatment or even for a purely sympathetic approach. Herbst seems to have implied by what she left behind all she wanted known about herself, although it was a story she could not bring herself to tell. There is no cover-up. The biographer has served her subject more effectively than fulsomely.

Why is a biography written? It is useful for the reviewer to ferret that fact out of the text—or the subtext. Do we need five-volume biographies that necessarily devote many pages to a few years? In Joseph Frank's multivolumed and magisterial (according to most critics) *Dostoevsky* (1977–), still short of completion, we find the writer at pains to deny that he is writing a conventional biography. "My interest in Dostoevsky's personal life is strictly limited," he insists. Frank nevertheless must sometimes suspend his exhaustive examination of the historical and cultural context from which the writings emerged, and his painstaking analysis of the writings themselves, because things happened to his hero, and his hero happened to do things himself, except in years in prison when he did no writing. But little documentation of the prison period exists, and Frank must focus on his subject's mind rather than his life in the army or in a prison cell, which can only be inferred from later writings, or the parallel accounts of contemporaries. Was Frank's interest in the minutiae of Dostoevsky's personal life limited, or was the documentation of that life limited? One can assume from what he has been able to re-create of his subject's physical and mental states that he would have done much with a few tantalizing tidbits. For Frank they would have been more than exotic texture for color use. Perhaps his disclaimer reveals that he anticipated accusations of making bricks without straw.

Some biographies cannot summon up sufficient facts for a single volume. Charles Nicholl's *A Cup of News: The Life of Thomas Nashe* (1984), on the Elizabethan pamphleteer and playwright, forced Bernard Levin to wonder, "Is there really enough of Nashe for him to deserve a biography rather than a chapter in someone else's? . . . Sometimes Mr. Nicholl is hard-pressed. He offers, for instance, 14 pages of close textual and thematic analysis of a play, 'The Isle of Dogs,' of which not a single line apart from the title has survived in print or manuscript, and of which nothing at all is known: a considerable achievement." Yet, because the Elizabethan context is colorfully full, the reviewer must add, "Nashe comes alive in Mr. Nicholl's hands, and in doing so demands to be taken seriously." Still, the question must be asked—is the work padded out to a book rather than a chapter in someone else's biography because the author had a contract to write a book? The shelves of the world's libraries are full of such empty biographies. Why did Nicholl chance his risky subject?

The critic of biography automatically views with suspicion all lives written by people with obvious axes to grind. Widows, sons and daughters, mothers, bosom or estranged friends, employees and accomplices, discarded mistresses. . . . Still, the fact of relationship is not necessarily a disabling element. Susan Cheever's *Home before Dark: A Biographical Memoir of John Cheever* (1984) is a painfully honest and sensitively written example. She knew her father well, had easy access to his letters and journals, and was willing to bare his torments, feeling that truth was the best advocate of his reputation, and that a sleazy and piecemeal revelation of his secret lives would do him even more posthumous harm.

Posthumous harm seems exactly the *intent* in Anthony West's *Aspects of a Life* (1984), where West, who had previously attacked his natural father, H. G. Wells, in his fiction, determined to bring down the reputation of his mother, Rebecca West, before the authorized biography in progress by Victoria Glendinning emerged to canonize her, as West apparently feared. Thus Wells now appears as warm-hearted father and visionary writer, rather than caddish and journalistic philanderer; and Rebecca West, mistreated mistress in the version of her life she permitted Gordon Ray to write based on information and letters she supplied, now appears, in her son's lens, a distorter of the facts. One must ask why Anthony West is interested in airing the linen between which his unwed parents slept, and why he did not rush to defend the abused and exploited mother against the uncaring and exploiting father. Since West wants us to see a self-dramatizing and dishonest woman who has fabricated her story at the expense of a likeable man who needed a flexibility of lifestyle to facilitate his creativity, one cannot help but question the motives of such biography, possibly even to suspect the materials on which it is based, as they are largely the memories of the writer and his paraphrases of alleged documentary sources.

Documentation itself is not truth. One must read a letter in the light of its intended audience, a diary entry in the light of the mental state in which it was written, the angle of perception of the viewer. The literal accuracy of the words themselves usually cannot be questioned when the source is described as accessible in a public collection. Invention here would be easily exposed. (Paraphrase of inaccessible material may be necessary because of permissions or copyright problems, but one must respect the paraphraser to accept the paraphrase.) Yet West raises an interesting question for the biographical critic by accusing his mother of fabricating letters and even diaries in support of her claims. Manuscripts and even printed books have a physical authenticity—even a fix in time—that can be checked, if one can get at them. Thomas J. Wise's Victorian forgeries and the recent "Hitler" forgeries prove that. Still, we seldom question such authenticity, despite our knowing that manuscripts can and will be faked and forged, even by the writer himself (or, in this alleged case, herself). Norman Douglas, when on his uppers during and after World War II, I was told by Michael Ayrton, would—for a paying customer—rewrite his lost and discarded old manuscripts by copying from the printed texts, and then "ageing" the paper in an oven. Thus were created new "original" manuscripts. He was his own forger, and he saw no harm in it. And he needed the money. Still, such dishonest copies mask the creative process.

It is a bewildering business, then, to be continuously on one's critical guard from so many angles. The biographer, the subject, the people around the subject who have something to gain or lose, each may affect the way the life story is refracted. And unless the book bears implicit cautionary warnings in it, as with West's *H. G. Wells*, we quickly lose sight of our need to be inherently skeptical, caught up as we may be in the style or the story.

The biography that seems to pry too much, for the sake, perhaps, of the scandal it evokes, is immediately suspect. Yet there are slick ways to evoke the same results that can look circumspect indeed. R. W. B. Lewis in his *Edith Wharton* (1975) put Mrs. Wharton's steamy, unfinished story about father-daughter incest not in the text but in an appendix, complete—literally making it easier to get at. It became the tail that wagged the dog, and copped most of the headlines. Almost certainly the book (which won a Pulitzer Prize) sold thousands more copies, and garnered far more publicity—provocative publicity at that—because of the seemingly discreet (yet actually discrete) placement strategy. (After all, no one reads appendixes! But critics were quick to spot the sensation.)

Writing about *A Portrait of Fryn* (1984), a biography of English novelist F. Tennyson Jesse (the laureate was her great-uncle), Victoria Glendinning observed that "the result of only half-comprehending the disaster areas in Fryn's life is that we do precisely seem to be peering through a 'half-open door'; the best argument for candid, even for 'intrusive' biography is that the half-seen seems so infinitely more disturbing than anything that is fully examined." (Jesse thought of titling her never-finished memoirs "The Half-Open Door.") A critic on the watch for the half-opened door will want to explore whether the partial opening is strategy or lack of data. Is there a sense of strain apparent at that stage of the narrative? How much does the writer about T. S.

Eliot care to say, given the data available, about Jean Verdenal? Or about Eliot's postseparation relationships with his first wife? How much does the writer about Henry James want to say about James's more-than-avuncular letters, in his old age, to young men? Or about the sexual orientation of some of those young men? The list can go on almost indefinitely, autobiographers needing far more skeptical scrutiny than biographers. Vladimir Nabokov even wrote his autobiography twice, using different "facts."

It helps to create an atmosphere of absolute honesty, whether in autobiography or biography. I was willing to accept anything I could not check out elsewhere after playwright Peter Nichols wrote in his engaging memoir, *Feeling You're Behind* (1984), that he wet his bed until he was seventeen, and that when he was in military service in India he was never tempted to touch Indian food. Trivial things, perhaps, but they compel acceptance of the rest. A sense of strain in handling embarrassing situations, on the other hand, leaves me uneasy about the entire book. When Irvin Ehrenpreis, concluding his massive, three-volume *Swift: The Man, His Works, and the Age* (1984), declares as Swift dodders into his last, dark years, that "the myth of a daemonic Swift was already passing into this world from the crooked inventions of remote tattlers," one senses that the biographer is uncomfortable about the medical facts of Swift's tormenting close. On the other hand, a happily chosen anecdote which encapsulates a life captures the critic in me. We are told in Peter Heyworth's *Otto Klemperer: His Life and Times* (1984) that the great conductor's teacher Hans Pfitzner believed passionately in *Werktreue*—fidelity to the work—and communicated that total identification with the work to his pupil not by exhortation but by example. When, during the second act of *Die Meistersinger*, it was evident that the singer playing Beckmesser was too ill to continue, Pfitzner handed his baton to an assistant. Then he went backstage and had himself shaved and made up, and went on stage to play the role in the final act. One can then understand the lasting influence of Pfitzner on Klemperer. Even if the story were not true (if it were not so, it should have been!), it suggests an authenticity of character that is compelling. The function of even fictitious contemporary anecdotes to convey an authenticity to a reputation is substantial, when confirming a character already established by the biographer.

Bare (no pun here) facts can be much less convincing. Ted Morgan in *Churchill* (1982) begins, "Spanked into life like the rest of us, Winston Leonard Spencer-Churchill was born on Monday, November 30, 1874, in Blenheim Palace." This looks like nothing but facts. We are to be drawn into the biography with that convincing feeling about everything else that follows. But was young Winston indeed spanked into life? Did his *accoucheur* find it necessary, or is Morgan assuming so from general obstetrical practice? Here, then, we begin with a vivid supposition presented as fact. The cautious critic will be skeptical, then, not merely about the cuteness of the opening, but its possible untruthfulness. Imaginary pictures, like imagined conversations, turn me off. Not much later the biographer tells us that Mrs. Everest, the nanny to whom Winston would be devoted, took charge of his toilet training. "She held his penis while he urinated, and washed it for him afterwards." Since it was in the nature of nannies to do so, did Morgan invent his memorable "fact"? And what does the presumably charming detail add, or signify, other than minor titillation? T. E. Lawrence had once written to Churchill himself about his *Marlborough* (1934) that he missed "the vivid, irrelevant petty detail which illumines. . . . I wish you had more care for trifles, sometimes. A triviality that has survived a long while is [often] more important than . . . contemporary events." But not a newly coined triviality which demeans subject and biographer. The cautious reviewer, the careful reader, will recognize such touches, and judge accordingly.

Since the biographer, regardless of the richness or the poverty of his sources, must regularly intervene among his materials to choose the compelling facts and the evocative details that converge at the angle of perception from which he wants the reader to view his subject, the biographer's own subjectivity—for a life is a work of art—is the subtle subtext of his book. How that perspective is first perceived, and then maintained, is the unending mystery of the biographer's art. Seeking it, Pamela Hansford Johnson once wrote, in reviewing a life of Frederick Rolfe ("Baron Corvo"), that if the subject's "*daimon*, [or at least] a thread of it, is not in the nature of the biographer, the resultant book cannot be wholly satisfactory." Such rapport should resonate from the opening lines, and should be consistent to the last, creating an ambience that commercial lives can rarely if ever achieve. Beyond documentation and balance and style, becoming attuned to a subject's *daimon* reconciles scholarship, psychology, and art. Can we sophisticate our critical attennae to recognize it?

Angus Easson

Reviewing Editions:
Letters, Journals,
Diaries

Reviews of literary letters, journals, and diaries are essentially of three kinds: the occasioned; the literary-critical; and the bibliographical.

The first, the reviewer's opportunity to write his essay on the author, is not dealt with here. It is often entertaining, critically valuable even, as a general scrutiny or evaluation; essentially, though, the edition is an excuse, the occasion not the concern of the review.

The second, which may in some degree overlap with the first, as it may also with the third, addresses itself specifically to the edition's contents. It asks about the literary consequences, historical and biographical as well as critical, for the author or for the body of material presented, as a direct result of this edition. How is our view of Wordsworth, for example, changed by having Beth Darlington's edition of his and his wife's "love" letters? Or of Gissing as man and novelist by having his diaries first given in full? Or of Elizabeth Gaskell as letter writer when offered her letters complete in effectively the first edition of them at all?[1] Such a review therefore opens new perspectives, themselves explicit or implicit in the editor's work, whether upon the author, including biographical and literary historical lights, or upon the author's canon. Here, the very issue of whether the edition was worth doing could be raised: might an article with quotations or a checklist have been more useful? Does the author or these letters or this diary justify the effort?

A question of value, different in kind yet no less vital, lies with the third kind of review, which explores the principles and practices of the edition. At the simplest level, it asks how accurate is the text, how useful is the apparatus? Has it been done well or—an issue of particular concern, since the superseding of a major bad edition in this field, soon or at all, by a major good one is unlikely—has it produced no good scholarly results, muddying the stream, betraying the author and the standards of scholarship? In earlier centuries, it could be argued, modern scrupulosity was not demanded or gave way to piety or discretion. Neither should have been a factor in the Brontë correspondence, the most obviously bad major edition that has not been nor is in process of being replaced: indeed, the recent reprinting of Wise and Symington's work makes a new edition even more remote. The low standard here was compounded by Wise's dispersal of the Brontë manuscripts, any future edition therefore having to cope with the problem of winkling out many manuscripts hoarded by individuals who are difficult to trace and often reluctant to let their treasures be seen. The danger of such bad editions is exemplified by Winifred Gérin's use of the Brontë correspondence, when, describing Charlotte and Anne's London visit of July 1848, Gérin has them walk through a snowstorm to Keighley, a phenomenon, Gérin says, which "was but the culmination of a summer of ceaseless rain . . . which at these altitudes has an unseasonable habit of falling as snow." Her ingenious gloss would have been unnecessary if Wise and Symington had been accurate, for Charlotte's original letter specifies a "thunderstorm."[2] Since the geographical dispersion of letters makes access to the originals difficult and expensive, and since, unlike poetry or other imaginative works, new editions are unusual, the highest standards of reliability should be demanded: a literary-critical review should make some assessment of accuracy, while a bibliographical review should set out the edition's strength and weakness, and may indeed be an important supplement to it.

The edition itself inevitably determines much about the review's nature. Since our concern is with scholarly reviewing, it is unlikely that primarily popular selections, like Trudy Bliss's of Jane Welsh Carlyle's letters, readable and welcome as that is, will normally be in question, nor even volumes drawn from standard editions, like Alan G. Hill's two selections of the letters of William and of Dorothy Wordsworth, where the text has already been established and, the aim being a wider readership, little new is offered beyond an introduction. These can be dealt with in brief critical notices. More marginal is a volume like Chapple and Sharps's *Elizabeth Gaskell: A Portrait in Letters*, which while chiefly offering a readable sequence of letters from the scholarly edition and supplying a linking commentary to form a biography, does reorder the letters and incorporate new material (frustratingly not distinguished: the reader is made to work hard in that respect).[3] On the other hand, Beth Darlington's edition of the Wordsworth "love" letters, while popular in format and aiming for a wider readership than most scholarly editions, is yet deserving of the fullest attention, partly on the basis of first publication, partly on that of the letters' intrinsic interest, and not least for its scrupulous presentation. *Cucullus non facit monachum*: and if Darlington's title smacks slightly of Book-of-the-Month Club, possibly concealing the value of what lies within, we should also be on the alert for work in full academic fig that is trivial or pretentious.

Since the nature of the work will condition the reviewer's approach, it is useful to consider, in broad terms, the main classes into which these works fall and what are, in the task of evaluation, their determining characteristics. If my opening three categories of review, even allowing for (often marked) overlap, bordered on the neo-Aristotelian, then classification of the kinds of letters and journals that offer themselves for review would demand not the Stagirite but Polonius himself: amongst them may be distinguished those of literary interest by the literary; of nonliterary interest by the literary; of literary interest by the nonliterary; even, of nonliterary interest (or no interest) by the nonliterary.

The first class includes letters like those of Elizabeth Gaskell or Dickens or George Eliot or Thackeray, which, besides other importance, all have literary merit, whether it lies in Gaskell's ability to suggest writing to the moment, a constant verbal movement giving the effect of someone engaged in talk; or in Dickens's to create a brilliant construction out of the observed world. And these letters, since their writers are also important literary figures, form part of a literary corpus, extending our understanding of it, and they also illuminate the creative processes, whether in descriptions of the very circumstances of writing, with Gaskell scribbling away during family holidays or standing at a mantelpiece as writing desk in Mary Mohl's Paris apartment, or by registering the pressures that in some measure underlie production, such as Thackeray's marriage and loving concern for his daughters, or else the rage and frustration at an army's destruction in the Crimea, which Dickens was to convert into the satire of the Circumlocution Office and the ideological underpinning of *Little Dorrit*. Such letters present few problems to the reviewer, once he has decided whether to evaluate the letters or to explore their significance for biography or literary history.

Other letters, however, those of my second class, afford a greater challenge. These are documents that in themselves might merit scant attention, yet are important because of their writers' literary status. The first volume of Hardy's letters covers 1840–92 and sees him through the publication of all his novels except *Jude*; the equally long-lived Tennyson is taken to 1850 and into his fifth decade by the first volume of his. In neither case would the literary merit alone of these volumes' contents warrant their publication. We must beware, it is true, of misjudging the ability of a letter writer because the evidence has been destroyed: after all, Tennyson, virulent against those who published private letters, urged others to burn and himself burnt correspondence. Such a consideration, though, does not make the extant papers any better as literature and it is dangerous to praise writers for hypothetical beauties. In the end, the slimness of the respective first volumes of Hardy's and Tennyson's letters has as little to do with destruction as does the merit of what survives. Some people enjoy writing letters; others direct their main literary energies elsewhere. Hardy's correspondence up to 1892 is chiefly on business matters, so giving, as his editors note (1:ix), the "sense not only of privacy but almost of impersonality" in sections of the first volume. Even in the wider and more expansive correspondence of his later years, caution is the predominant effect. Hardy's letters are documents rather than literature, important because of Hardy, not because of themselves. Even more, Tennyson stands as one who hated writing letters: once married, most of his correspondence was conducted by his wife and, later, by his son Hallam: he "would claim that he needed his energy for writing poetry and that he would as soon kill a pig as write a letter," an attitude that led FitzGerald, a truly great letter writer, to lament that "Alfred himself never writes, nor indeed cares a halfpenny about one."[4] As documents, Tennyson's letters are important, as are his proxy letters written by Emily, Lady Tennyson, yet they can scarcely be reviewed on their intrinsic merits. They demand to be handled, like those of Hardy, with some demonstration of how they function as documents, in the context of the poet's life and work.

In a class by themselves are those letters and diaries (this second a particularly fruitful category), produced by people not otherwise writers. Jane Welsh Carlyle is a classic example: there is nothing literary other than the letters and they are wonderfully entertaining and deeply moving. Until recently it was fashionable to denigrate her husband's letters in comparison with her natural style and lively particularity of detail, and it may be that Thomas Carlyle will never be seen as a great *letter* writer, central though he is to our understanding of the nineteenth century. It will be interesting to see the effect upon the Carlyles of their correspondence being issued jointly: it is reasonably advanced now (nine volumes to date, taking us up to 1837), even if the venture seems to have provoked less interest than, say, the Pilgrim Dickens. Edward FitzGerald, though his claim to literary fame may seem lodged in the *Rubáiyát*, is another whose letters, long enjoyed in selections and now fully available, stand as his true achievement. Such writers need to have their literary value assessed and their letters considered as a body of work, just as Dorothy Wordsworth establishes herself as a writer through her journals. (The letters give her a further claim to attention.) Whether she really ever will be established as a poet, as Susan Levin has sought to do, is a moot point; however, whatever canonical revision Dorothy may undergo, the journals will retain their literary preeminence as well as their importance as adjuncts to our understanding of Dorothy's brother and of Coleridge.[5] Dorothy of course has extrinsic importance because of her circle, as Jane Carlyle has because of her husband, whereas diarists like Thomas Turner of East Hoathly or Woodforde or Kilvert give us access to a world essentially revealed only through their work. Turner's account of a small shopkeeper's life is fascinating and often comical as social history: "We continued, drinking like horses, as the vulgar phrase is, and singing till many of us were very drunk, and then we went to dancing and pulling wigs, caps, and hats, and thus we continued in this frantic manner, behaving more like mad people than they that profess the name of Christians" (7 March 1758). We need, though, to consider how it is that that life exists in the account Turner gives. A third type of person in this class is the man or woman whose journal or letters confer literary status, while that person also has claims outside the literary field, whether as civil servant, teacher, scientist, politician, or whatever. Discussion here would presumably accommodate a career such as that of Pepys as servant to the state.

On the face of it, the fourth division, work of no literary interest produced by nonliterary people, is unlikely to come our way, though such does exist. Gladstone's diaries are an outstanding example: these bald records of letters written, meetings attended, business done, books read, and cryptic references to streetwomen helped, attach themselves vitally to all else that we know of Gladstone's life: the edition is essential to historians— and even to those who edit literary letters. Yet it is difficult to believe anyone could read these volumes for their literary merit. More within the province of the literary reviewer is something like the edition of John Wordsworth's letters, where his brother makes the literary connection. William called John a "*silent* poet"; he never wrote anything imaginative and his letters show, despite the occasional intriguing comment ("The poem of the Wye is a poem that I admire but after having read it I do not like to turn to it again" [p. 156]), how little his talents lay in writing, though for light on the Wordsworth circle and with their warmth of affection as well as sense of business they are good to have.

As well as the form and nature of the work itself, what is written will be shaped by the academic journal commissioning the review plus any brief from the editor (nature; length; urgency); and by the reviewer's knowledge and inclinations. It may seem rather late to consider the reviewer's qualifications at this stage. After all, if the journal editor has asked you to review the book and you have got this far in preparation, such consideration, one way or another, is superfluous. But the reviewer, in mentally shaping up to writing, should be aware of what can reasonably be expected of him.

Clearly, the state of studies of an author and of editions already available must be known and taken into account. The edition of Gaskell's letters was pioneering work, since with the exception of the correspondence with Charles Eliot Norton, little had been printed before, despite the able use made by A. B. Hopkins of manuscript materials in *Elizabeth Gaskell: Her Life and Work* (1952). On the other hand, Dickens's letters, quite apart from extensive quotation in John Forster's life of Dickens (1872–74), have gone through a variety of editions since the collection made by his sister-in-law and daughter, culminating, before the Pilgrim project, with the three volumes in the Nonesuch Dickens. When the Pilgrim edition began to appear in the 1960s, then, Dickens's letters were not an unknown quantity. What the Pilgrim general editors have done, on the foundation laid by Humphry House, is to gather every possible letter, to establish the best texts, and to provide the fullest of commentaries. Our approach to reviewing Dickens's letters will accordingly differ from that to the Gaskell volume, while always bearing in mind extraliterary factors: access to the Nonesuch Dickens, for example, has always been limited by the edition being confined to 877 sets. Again, the edition of Wordsworth's letters that is currently in progress is a recension of Ernest de Selincourt's original work: while offering better texts and many new ones, the difficulty such an edition, important as it is, presents to ill-equipped reviewers, especially in popular rather than scholarly contexts, appears by a shuffling stance which arises from not knowing what can be said beyond a resumé of Wordsworth's life in the period covered by the volume under review.

The qualifications of the reviewer who can make something new and interesting out of such tasks will include a wide yet detailed knowledge of the author; of the author's circle; of related authors; and of the period in general; together with a fair knowledge of bibliography and editing if a critical review is intended or of criticism, if a bibliographical one. The reviewer should be capable or have experience of being an editor, yet not be a bitter or frustrated one. If this seems as much good (or obvious) advice about editing as about reviewing, it follows because the good reviewer here is a mirror image of the good editor: one should be, in the best sense, a match for the other. And what follows, I suspect, may sound as much "Instructions to an Editor" as to a reviewer.

"Shaping up" to writing was mentioned above, and in my experience the leading ideas and general form of the review begin to emerge during the initial reading. One concern that may be relevant to the very nature of the review, indeed be openly discussed in it, is the issue, already averted to, of literary value. People who have no difficulty with novels, plays, epics, sonnets, lyrics, even fragments, seem rattled when faced by a letter or a diary. Clearly, these writings raise critical questions of intention, consciousness, genre, and form, yet there is surely no doubt that they can have literary value: a letter is shaped, a diary is the product of a conscious mind, even when seen, as in some of Coleridge's notebook entries, to be little more than idling. The idea of organic form, the creative use of language, the human revelation of idea and feeling are all as surely qualities of these writings as of any others. That reference to "human revelation" points up another stumbling block, perhaps felt the more strongly given some current critical issues. Those to whom the idea of the text as an independent, even free-floating form has come as a revelation often seek to deny the meaningful connection of a work with the author or with life itself. Certainly, no one wants excess intentionality or the idea that the work is only of interest as a biographical or psychological adjunct to its author. But art, separate entity though it is from life (no revelation to some of us), still must derive from and feed back into life or else the sense of play so stressed of recent years (and certainly valuable as a critical concept) becomes meaningless, a trivial swapping of verbal counters. Letters or journals must be assessed in themselves; they should also be related, where appropriate, to the author's other work and, where appropriate, to the author's life, all with that tact which is an essential quality of scholar or critic. Paradoxically, in making literary judgments, the reviewer of letters and journals may claim the writings he is reviewing (as against the edition) are valueless and yet still say they have value or interest in the context of the author's life or work. Gissing's diary entry of 3 September 1896 ("A fine day. Did 3 pp.") has, despite brevity and the ring of truth, minimal literary merit: taken, however, as part of the cumulative effect of how he slogged away, in this instance at *The Whirlpool*, it reveals much about Gissing's determination as a working novelist. These ideological issues may or may not be treated in the review: they will, however, necessarily be in the mind of the reviewer, who has, in this respect, complex problems not given to the reviewer of other kinds of imaginative literature or of criticism or of literary history.

In the practicalities of the review, the reviewer will be aware of and bear in mind at all times certain distinct and different problems of, on the one hand, editions of letters and, on the other, journals and diaries. With letters, their survival is often arbitrary, depending amongst other things on the recipient and on the writer's fame. Dickens was famous in his early twenties, besides being a prolific correspondent, so Boz's letters were preserved in large numbers: yet Dickens, like many of his contemporaries, urged the destruction of personal correspondence and himself more than once had epistolary bonfires. Survival can be deceptive if we interpret it as indicative of the importance and intensity of relationships. Of Dickens's letters to H. F. Chorley a mere handful survive, suggesting a lack of intimacy apparently confirmed by John Forster's life of Dickens, in which Chorley plays a subordinate role. Yet Chorley has been claimed, with some justice, as one of the closest friends of Dickens's later years.[6] Chorley observed in his obituary notice of Dickens (*Athenaeum*, 18 June 1870) that Dickens always asked that his letters be destroyed: a wish that Chorley himself fulfilled in a bonfire of personal correspondence. He blotted himself out, so far as an edition of Dickens's letters is concerned, and a reviewer must be aware of such blanks. Again, letters survive but with varying degrees of accessibility for the prospective editor: those in public collections, even if widely distributed, can be traced, but others are carefully guarded or not even recognized by their owners. To stand, as I have done, in a pub in Richmond, Surrey, with a gin and tonic, surreptitiously transcribing a Dickens letter framed on the wall may be unnecessarily self-dramatizing: no reason why the owners should have objected to transcription; but they certainly were not aware of the Pilgrim editors' search for such material. Each new volume of the Pilgrim Dickens prompts new finds, and in some degree all judgments must be provisional, since they may be modified or even overturned by unexpected discoveries such as the Wordsworth "love" letters. Letters, of course, are to correspondents. More often than not only one side is preserved, while a writer will modify tone and material according to the recipient, so presenting different sides or different masks: one of the delights of FitzGerald as letter writer is his ability to vary the same material according to his correspondent. Sometimes, therefore, we have only a few of a range of voices. And if the writer modifies voice to fit the recipient, in what sense do we have the truth? We might adapt Dr. Johnson's declaration and say that no man is on oath in his letters: the reviewer, recognizing that truth may be colored or even concealed, must be alert to tone and have the knowledge to see round or through the letters, as well as testing the guidance the edition provides in this respect. If it is rare for a complete correspondence to survive (and anything like completeness may itself be a problem, as witness the wonderful if daunting editions of Horace Walpole's and Voltaire's correspondence), the issue remains of how complete an edition of correspondence should aim to be. A minor figure may not seem to justify a full edition (and presumably wouldn't sell it): anyone, however important, the bulk of whose correspondence consists of—"My dear sir, I regret I cannot, Yours sincerely"—is going to be hard to get into print. Yet we may also remember what Humphry House said in 1951 about why the Dickens letters aimed to be complete: for a writer so important every scrap, every note however seemingly trivial, added to our understanding.[7] Just to print everything possible enlarges our sense of the energy of the man. Dickens justifies completeness because of his literary stature and because of intrinsic merit; FitzGerald justifies completeness because of intrinsic merit—there is hardly a dud in the four volumes. And when the cost of producing an edition is so immense that it seems unlikely to be done again, better to have too much than too little. Some editions, that of Clough, for example, seek an alternative by giving a checklist of known correspondence and printing the most interesting. The reviewer will give these considerations play according to the content and the editorial principles of the edition in hand.

The distinctive problems of journals and diaries include (again) survival, though their nature makes it less common for them to be widely dispersed. Still, three volumes of John Chapman's diaries, for 1851, 1860, and 1863, turned up on a bookstall in Sneinton Market, Nottingham, while the rest (supposing they existed) are still lost to sight.[8] Diaries, if destroyed, tend to be destroyed outright, though intermediate cases crop up, like the deletions in Dorothy Wordsworth's Grasmere Journal, blottings out that have led to speculation (often misguided) as to what they conceal—and to at least one ill-judged academic joke.[9] Assiduous diarists may keep up the practice for much of their lives and this bulk is often a problem, unless the subject is of major importance (Gladstone, again) or the diary itself is a major work (Pepys's, most famously, which has at last received its full due in an edition that caters expertly to an audience both academic and general). Certainly, the argument is all in favor of a complete edition where possible, so that a document is made available: followed if required by a more popular volume of selections. Doubt has been evident whether Fanny Burney, for instance, justified intrinsically or extrinsically the fine edition of her letters and journals: Pat Rogers, however, reviewing the final volumes, wrote of how the edition "has already enhanced Fanny's reputation as a chronicler and observer of real life" (as he notes, her account of a mastectomy in 1811 [6:596ff.] has achieved a kind of classic status), and he wondered "whether the letters will allow us to smuggle Fanny Burney into a more central place in literary history."[10]

After issues of survival and length, the nature of journals prompts the reviewer to the question of why they are kept. Many reviewers, keeping their own, will have answers for themselves. Dorothy Wordsworth kept her Grasmere Journal initially and partially because it would give William pleasure when he returned (14 May 1800); Pepys's diary, his most recent editors suggest, is a concomitant of his delight in bookkeeping (1:cvi), with some enforcement from the spiritual and moral totting-up of Protestant written self-examination; Gissing, again, relieved something of his misery through his, and was prompted to take it up again in April 1902 after the lapse of nearly a year as a result of rereading the first volume: "such strange and moving reading." Self-preservation; the hope of a memorial; and yet also the truth about oneself, however distasteful, known only to oneself in life and to others only after one's death: these are amongst the motives for keeping diaries, and though not directed to an obvious and certain audience, some idea of a reader or listener, however vague, however shifting, lies in the journal and should accordingly be borne in mind, even to the recognition that the writer may portray his worst or weakest side in the throes of misery or self-castigation.

Whatever kind of review is being written, always read all the preliminaries carefully. The advice is obvious but it can save a world of troubles, not least in avoiding the editor's irate or pained correspondence, brought on you by failure to do so. Besides, these are an essential test of the edition's soundness. At a pinch some of the notes might be skipped and anyone can be excused from combing through every index entry. The preliminaries, however, set out (and if not, it is a mark against the edition) the editorial principles of inclusion, transcription, presentation, and bibliographical information provided, together with an indication of the audience aimed for. Editorially self-imposed limitations should be noted and assessed. The question then arises, to be tested by the body of the text, whether these preliminaries serve to make, and succeed in making, the edition usable: the answer can only come after close acquaintance and detailed use of the work, but the reviewer, aware of this, will devise tests, based on information in the preliminaries, to try the editor's work. Some preliminaries are slight. Beth Darlington, in half a page (p. 9) on the handling of her Wordsworth texts, effectively covers her practice, which itself can draw upon the model of the collected Wordsworth correspondence; the brevity serves also to define the combined scholarly and general readership for which Darlington successfully aims. Pepys's diary, on the other hand, equally designed for a dual readership, gives twenty-seven pages (1:xli-lxvii) to an account of the manuscript, the shorthand, and the text. Again, Darlington's edition, for all its care, is in some sort an interim measure, designed to make available the essential material until it can be incorporated with the standard edition; the Pepys diary aims (as far as anything can in this mortal world) to be definitive. And so each edition must be understood in its individual terms. Together with the preliminaries, any general biographical or critical introduction should be investigated: claims for the edition's establishing biographical information or literary worth may help shape the review.

In turning to the text, the reviewer should be able to offer a detailed discussion of, or at very least an informed opinion on, the transcription: it is also advisable that all prospective reviewers in this field have at some time tried their hand at transcription (it can be a chastening exercise). Only a few people reviewing Pepys's diary will have experience of the Shelton system of shorthand: though any that have should give it full play, since at least one review ought to tell us how accurate, given difficulties of transcription and presentation of a text, this edition is. Most reviewers, though, should have a familiarity with the handwriting of the period and preferably of the author. Care is needed, though it is unlikely that any modern editor will be so careless of his simplest duties as Edmund Gosse was in his Gray letters, where he falsely claimed to have newly transcribed the letters to Wharton: Gosse had, in fact, set someone else to transcribe the letters for him, who, discovering they had previously been published, began to copy from the printed versions; Gosse then failed to check these "transcriptions" against the originals.[11] Access to manuscripts is often difficult: if so, checking may have to be on a limited scale. Most editions, however, reproduce a page or more of their originals, while it is sometimes possible to check from photographs in other works. John Forster's letter to W. J. Fox, partially transcribed in the Pilgrim Dickens (4: 235, n. 6), is reproduced in Richard Renton's *John Forster and His Friendships* (London, 1912; opposite p. 210), which shows that an ampersand got left out. This is a slight enough slip, and it is no business of the reviewer to crow over the discovery. Somewhat more worrying, though, is the evidence in FitzGerald's letters of a misreading of "setting" for "settling" (3:315; Ms. reproduced 3:317), which influences the sense of a passage, while earlier the evident failure (1:122) to transcribe "Castara" correctly (the printed text reads "Castra") leads to a puzzled note, which in turn suggests no very good editorial grasp of early seventeenth-century poetry, since the context, including Phineas Fletcher's *The Purple Island*, makes it clear that William Habington's poems were meant. Even these two errors may be insignificant; they might, however, alert the reviewer to the need for a closer investigation of the transcription's accuracy. Such examples, it may also without cynicism be noted, help to establish the real care with which the reviewer has treated the text, and errors should be taken as symptoms rather than disease: significant error in the sample is what to look for, not the occasional human error: the Pilgrim Dickens's texts (I speak as one annotating half of volume 7, but not involved in establishing the texts) have been checked and rechecked with scrupulous care, while the general standard of the FitzGerald letters is clearly good. Scholars, critics, and readers reasonably expect a scholarly edition to be accurate in its basics, and the kind of problems caused by inaccuracy have been illustrated by Gérin's misfortune in relying upon the slovenly Brontë correspondence. It is the legitimate business of the reviewer to test the goodness of the text and lay bare evidence of serious inaccuracy or carelessness.

Editions that combine letters and journals—those of Fanny Burney, Byron, and George Eliot are notable examples—may require consideration of how such parallel material is presented. Should the journal(s) be printed separately and continuously, or should journal material (in the case of George Eliot, from Lewes and Chapman amongst others as well as Eliot herself) be inserted into the chronological run of letters? The former course seems to me the preferable one, though there is no doubt that diaries can interconnect importantly with letters when read in parallel and such integration may avoid burdensome cross-reference. For scholarly purposes, one would prefer the diary complete and in unbroken sequence: Haight inserts substantial extracts from George Eliot's extant journals, but his primary concern is with the correspondence, however much not giving the journals complete may have been an opportunity lost. On the other hand, many of the Fanny Burney journals were really diary-letters, designed for and sent to specific correspondents, while some of the later journals incorporate letters or were arranged by Burney herself into sequence with her correspondence. The editorial and critical issues here will be picked up according to an edition's individual nature. Quite another problem of ordering (happily rare) is raised by the arrangement of the Gaskell letters: here, a large batch came to hand when the edition was already set up. One may regret, even while grateful that these letters did surface, that it proved impossible to insert them into the main sequence, though the numbering of items assists the reader in reordering them. The reviewer, faced by such a situation, can really do little beyond regretting the necessity of the arrangement, welcoming the letters' availability, and expressing a pious hope for an early revised second edition.

Different editions provide various kinds of bibliographical information. Most have the obvious details of dating, correspondent, source, postmarks, and address: others also give watermarks, indication of previous publication (if any), nature of paper (color, dimension, foliation). There may be problems here: in the FitzGerald letters one item is printed twice (2:123 and 176), with only place of writing changed: the chart shows they each stem from a Cambridge manuscript; the explanation is not clear, but something has passed undetected by the editors. How important all these details are will appear by use. Some editors place the information with the individual letter, as in the Dickens, for example, and the George Eliot: others consign it to the beginning or end of each volume. The decision is partly conditioned by editorial intention, though economics may play its part. Leslie Marchand's Byron is clearly aimed at a wide audience and offers the information at the end of each volume. The reviewer's judgment should be conditioned but not determined by such factors. The Byron edition works well; the Gaskell edition, vital for scholarship and delightful as the letters are, while offering more information, is tiresome to use, involving eight columns of data, three of which demand reference back to other appendixes, the width and closeness of the entries on the page making it difficult to read across without the aid of a ruler. Again, let me stress the value of the Gaskell edition; we cannot be without it; but on this as on other scores it is not the happiest of volumes to work with, and the reviewer's comments might make other editors, like Jacob with the angel, wrestle with their publishers in the task of production: good publishers, of course, have production editors skilled in page appearance and general book design.

As well as the bibliographical notes, which will demand particular attention in certain editions, or in a primarily bibliographical review, those that provide the annotation or commentary need careful assessment. A major edition should surely annotate thoroughly and helpfully. An increasing number of recent academic publications have been reprimanded for annotating the simplest things (foreign-language phrases that are an accepted part of English; London as the capital of England; etc.) and for yet still further compounding this by ignoring or misrepresenting essential or puzzling references. Two things are generally identified as the root of this problem: an increasing ignorance, in the assumed readership, of what in the past was taken as the common stock of an educated person; and an increasing ignorance in some academics, who nonetheless press on with editing. Most respectable editions assume some knowledge: of foreign phrases, and often of French, as well as of things like basic classical mythology and European history; and indeed of access to and familiarity with obvious works of reference like dictionaries, encyclopedias, and handbooks. Some castigation of inadequate or poor or obvious notes may be in order, especially if the real problems seem to be ignored. A legitimate difficulty arises from transatlantic culture and is effectively underlined by Gordon Haight in the George Eliot correspondence: "The vexing problem of what to leave unexplained cannot be solved to the complete satisfaction of readers on both sides of the Atlantic. Apple butter is familiar to most Americans, but damson cheese conveys not the slightest notions of plums or sweetness. A note on either will insult the intelligence of as many readers as it helps. In deciding whether to annotate or not I have tried to consider the general convenience" (1:xxxvi). Again, some authors need more elucidation than others; while some stand so in their own right or in relation to their age that they demand commentary of the most detailed kind. As well as extensive notes, the Pepys diary has a volume of commentary (vol. 10), while the annotation of Coleridge's notebooks, so wonderfully complex, occupies a separate volume from that of the text, thus facilitating the best use of what constitutes one of the age's greatest achievements of literary scholarship. Editions often provide biographical information separately, and to have important correspondents identified and sketched early on seems useful, as in both the George Eliot and the FitzGerald letters. The two prime tests of notes are accuracy and relevance. One can sometimes wonder whether an editor has lifted his eyes from the word or allusion to its context. Though out of my province, it may be allowed by way of tribute to Harold Jenkins's monumental Arden edition (1982) of *Hamlet*, to refer reviewers and editors to his explanation (and exploration) of "nunnery" (3.1.121 and pp. 493–96), where he eruditely and lucidly strips away established misconceptions and helps a new understanding of word, of dramatic situation and character, and of the play. Again, to use another example not strictly germane in this chapter, a note that "Demeter found her daughter, Persephone, at Eleusis, a scene depicted on classical vases" hardly helps explain the significance in the text of the character having "her great finger upon her lip, like the Eleusian priestess on the vase": the allusion to the Eleusian mysteries and the silence imperative upon the initiated needs bringing out rather than the reader being left no wiser (or indeed more confused) than before.[12] Notes that aim at literary criticism (the business of the introduction, if at all) do not help these editions, whereas those that provide commentary are often a guide through the material: the Coleridge letters pick up the first reference to opium and subsequently the first indication that drugs are being used on a regular basis to relieve mental distress (1:18, 188); on the other hand, FitzGerald's reference to Virgil as a homosexual—as I interpret the question "was he much of a b———?" (1:348)—receives no note: neither to expand "b———" or explain Virgil's sexual interests, whether as reported of his life or in, for example, the Eclogues with "that horrid one, / Beginning *Formosum Pastor Corydon*"; nor to introduce a surely necessary reference to FitzGerald's own emotional makeup. Indeed, the FitzGerald letters, fine though they are as a complete collection and illuminating though the biographical and topographical information is, seem the most problematic in their notes of editions I know that aim for fairly full annotation.[13] There is, for example, no consistency: some Shakespeare quotations are identified, others are not; while many literary allusions pass without comment, whether because ignored or simply not recognized is unclear. Elsewhere, information is wrong or absurd, while the opportunity for important commentary is lost. The notes also fail through trying to be too clever: this is the eager Scylla over against the engulfing Charybdis of dull pedantry, but the Fitz-Gerald notes on Ugolino and on Horace (3:398, 646), ingenious though they are, fail to show awareness of the standard allusions, in the first instance to Dante's account of Ugolino in the tower of famine, in the second to the *Art of Poetry*. Such weakness a reviewer may legitimately trace through, always with under-standing, never with ill-feeling or triumph.

The other great necessity in an edition is "The trouble of an index," as Marchand wittily calls his final Byron volume. In works of this description, even more than most, one inclines to agree with Carlyle that there should be no copyright protection for those unprovided with an index. Where an edition appears in several volumes, especially if issued over a period of years, it may be useful to comment on how the series is indexed. Volume 2 of Fanny Burney, for instance, carries the index for volumes 1 and 2; there is no index in the George Eliot correspondence until volume 7; other editions, amongst them the Byron and the Dickens letters, are indexed at the end of each volume: the final Byron volume is besides an integrated index. Whatever the reasons, it is often awkward—and downright frustrating if only the text volume has been borrowed from the library—to have no index in any one volume. Only recently has the indexer been regarded (like the lexicographer) as more than "a harmless drudge": the task required deserves full recognition. The good-ness of an index is only properly realized in constant and pro-longed use: again, a reviewer should deliberately consult it frequently and devise ways to discover its strengths and weak-nesses. The Gaskell letters, a collection I have used a good deal and always thankfully, fails in this. Its index has good intentions, and begins by being divided into three: Select Family Index; Literary Index; General Biographical Index, the first and second being subdivided. The first disappointment is the decision to index not by page but by letter number: presumably easier, in that it could be undertaken before page proof stage; but it makes progress difficult in the longer letters, which can be five or more pages of densely packed type that I find difficult to eye-scan. The second disappointment is the omissions that become apparent as the edition is used: in Index 2(a) at least two important references to *North and South* are excluded, while in 2(b), literary references outside Gaskell's works, *The Excursion* (and numerous shorter Wordsworth poems), Tennyson's "The Brook," the Essays of Macaulay, and Southey's *Life and Correspondence* receive no entry. In Index 3, apart from omissions and confusions (John Bright is indexed under Henry A. Bright), there are only the sparest biographical entries: try to find, for example, the occasion (p. 492) when Gaskell declared to Charles Eliot Norton that she felt medieval and un-Manchester: no help in Index 1 under Gaskell herself; it means combing through all the letters to Norton and is not easy then, given the length of most of them. To turn from this to the indexer of the Pilgrim Dickens or the Byron letters or the Burney letters and journals is to move into a difficult world. Even with these the basis is name and place, though with topics organized under names, and on occasions it would be useful to have separate entries under "dogs" or "ghosts" or "turnips, cultivation of": if we know Dickens had a dog called Timber, we can find him in, for example, volume 5, under his name, but if we want dogs of Dickens (or pets in general) there is no help, under either the main entry for Dickens or a separate subject entry. How detailed or itemized can an index be? Once subject entries are chosen as a basis, the index may begin to outrun the text. Certain decisions that make best sense must have been taken by editor and indexer and be recognized by the reviewer: in this sense the Pilgrim's index serves Dickens the writer and Dickens the society man rather than Dickens the man of opinions and character traits, in a sense because he is the edition, whereas others, for example Catherine Dickens, have topic entries for such things as social life and health, since they are lesser lights to his central luminary.

I may seem in this account to have concentrated unduly upon features of the bibliographical review; I may also seem to have emphasized the anecdotal or the isolated details rather than the larger issues. The literary-critical review, however, needs less specific considerations and its nature was, I hope, sufficiently brought out earlier, while my illustrations have stemmed from a concern for a diagnosis which itself should spring from careful reading and thought, not from any wish simply to amuse by a superficial account aiming to display only symptoms or (worse still) the reviewer's cleverness. In reaching some general conclusions, I would underline, first, that the editions here considered only yield their full significance through use; second, that the reviewer must recognize the dedicated and sometimes tedious work involved in good editing; third, that the reviewer has a duty to the work and the author that does not exclude castigating a bad edition; and fourth, that mere cleverness, as opposed to wit or readability or a sense of humor, is to be avoided. Coleridge's anecdote (*Letters*, 6:733) may be salutary: he had, he says, "written some half a score or more of what, I thought clever & epigrammatic & devilishly severe Reviews . . . but a Remark made by Miss Wordsworth, to whom I had in full expectation of gaining a laugh of applause read one of my Judgements occasioned my committing the whole Batch to the Fire." Eschew the merely clever or "devilishly severe," seek to serve the edition and the author, and in the process we may ourselves escape the burning.

Notes

1. For details of editions discussed, see the bibliography at the end of this essay; references in the text are to these editions by volume (where appropriate) and page.

2. Gérin, *Charlotte Brontë: The Evolution of Genius* (Oxford: Clarendon Press, 1967; rpt. London: Oxford Univ. Press, 1969), p. 360. The manuscript, in the John Rylands University of Manchester Library, is accurately reproduced in *Mary Taylor, Friend of Charlotte Brontë: Letters from New Zealand and Elsewhere*, ed. Joan Stevens (London: Oxford Univ. Press, 1972), pp. 175–81. Stevens points out C. K. Shorter's responsibility for the corrupt text (pp. 175–76). Gérin states (p. xiii) she has used but not trusted Wise and Symington and refers to the manuscript (p. 360n).

3. In the Pepys diary also new material is not distinguished: true, it might make seem odd in the future what is now the established text, but tracing through of earlier editorial treatment is thereby made that much more difficult.

4. Robert Bernard Martin, *Tennyson: The Unquiet Heart* (Oxford: Clarendon Press, 1980), pp. 85, 516.

5. For Dorothy Wordsworth as poet, see Susan Levin and Robert Ready, "Unpublished Poems from Dorothy Wordsworth's Commonplace Book," *Wordsworth Circle* 9 (1978):33–44; and Susan M. Levin, "Subtle Fire: Dorothy Wordsworth's Prose and Poetry," *Massachusetts Review* 21 (1980):345–63.

6. See the claim of Henry G. Hewlett, the editor of *Henry Fothergill Chorley: Autobiography, Memoir, and Letters*, 2 vols. (London: Richard Bentley, 1873), 2:326; and also the account in Robert Bledsoe, "Dickens and Chorley," *Dickensian* 75 (1979):157–66.

7. House, "A New Edition of Dickens's Letters," *All in Due Time* (London: Rupert Hart-Davis, 1955), and in particular pp. 225–28.

8. Gordon S. Haight, *George Eliot & John Chapman: With Chapman's Diaries* (New Haven: Yale Univ. Press, 1940), pp. ix–x. Haight prints the diaries for 1851 and 1860; that for 1861 vanished again: Haight notes what is known of its contents (p. 252).

9. See Jonathan Wordsworth's letter in the *TLS*, 21 May 1976, p. 614; it was part of an exchange begun by F. W. Bateson (9 April 1976, p. 430): Robert Woof's letter (28 May 1976, pp. 646–47) examines the textual problem seriously.

10. Rogers, "Miss Slyboots in Mayfair," *TLS*, 4 January 1985, p. 8. The Burney edition, full though it is, is not complete, since it only begins in 1791; it can be supplemented by the *Diary and Letters of Madame d'Arblay*, 7 vols. (London: Henry Colburn, 1842–46), and by *A Catalogue of the Burney Family Correspondence, 1749–1878*, comp. Joyce Hemlow (New York: New York Public Library, 1971).

11. See *Correspondence of Thomas Gray*, ed. Paget Toynbee and Leonard Whibley, rev. H. W. Starr, 3 vols. (Oxford: Clarendon Press, 1935; rpt. 1971), 1:xxi–xxii; for a description of a modern editor's care, see the account in *The Journals and Letters of Fanny Burney (Madame d'Arblay)*, ed. Joyce Hemlow, 12 vols. (Oxford: Clarendon Press, 1972–84), 1:xiii–xiv.

12. See Sheridan Le Fanu, *Uncle Silas*, ed. W. J. McCormack and Andrew Swarbrick (Oxford: Oxford Univ. Press, 1981), p. 19 and note.

13. My admiration for the edition is, I hope, clear from my review of the FitzGerald letters in *Literature and History* 9 (1983):246–49.

Bibliography of Editions Discussed

Boswell, James. *Boswell in Holland, 1763–1764*. Ed. Frederick A. Pottle. London: William Heinemann, 1952.

———. *Boswell's London Journal*. Ed. Frederick A. Pottle. London: William Heinemann, 1950.

The Brontës: Their Lives, Friendships & Correspondence. Ed. T. J. Wise and J. A. Symington. 4 vols. Oxford: Basil Blackwell, 1933. Reprinted, 4 vols. as 2, 1980.

Burney, Fanny. *The Journals and Letters of Fanny Burney (Madame D'Arblay)*. Ed. Joyce Hemlow et al. 12 vols. Oxford: Clarendon Press, 1972–1984.

Byron, George Gordon, Lord. *Byron's Letters and Journals*. Ed. Leslie A. Marchand. 12 vols. London: John Murray, 1973–1982.

Carlyle, Jane Welsh. *Jane Welsh Carlyle: A Selection of Her Letters*. Ed. Trudy Bliss. London: Victor Gollancz, 1950.

Carlyle, Thomas, and Jane Welsh. *The Collected Letters of Thomas and Jane Welsh Carlyle*. Duke-Edinburgh Edition. Ed. Charles Richard Sanders and K. J. Fielding. In progress. Durham, N.C.: Duke University Press, 1970–.

Clough, Arthur Hugh. *The Correspondence of Arthur Hugh Clough*. Ed. Frederick L. Mulhauser. 2 vols. Oxford: Clarendon Press, 1957.

Coleridge, Samuel Taylor. *Collected Letters of Samuel Taylor Coleridge*. Ed. Earl Leslie Griggs. 6 vols. Oxford: Clarendon Press, 1956–1971.

———. *The Notebooks of Samuel Taylor Coleridge*. Ed. Kathleen Coburn. In progress. New York: Pantheon Books, 1957–.

Dickens, Charles. *The Letters of Charles Dickens*. Ed. Georgina Hogarth and Mamie Dickens. 3 vols. London: Chapman and Hall, 1880–1882.

———. *The Letters of Charles Dickens*. Nonesuch Edition. Ed. Walter Dexter. 3 vols. London: Nonesuch Press, 1938.

———. *The Letters of Charles Dickens*. Pilgrim Edition. Ed. Madeline House, Graham Storey, and Kathleen Tillotson. In progress. Oxford: Clarendon Press, 1965–.

Eliot, George. *The George Eliot Letters*. Ed. Gordon S. Haight. 7 vols. New Haven: Yale University Press, 1954. 2 supplementary vols., 1978.

FitzGerald, Edward. *The Letters of Edward FitzGerald*. Ed. A. M. Terhune and Annabelle Burdick Terhune. 4 vols. Princeton: Princeton University Press, 1980.

Gaskell, Elizabeth. *Elizabeth Gaskell: A Portrait in Letters*. Ed. J. A. V. Chapple and John Geoffrey Sharps. Manchester: Manchester University Press, 1980.

———. *The Letters of Mrs. Gaskell*. Ed. J. A. V. Chapple and Arthur Pollard. Manchester: Manchester University Press, 1966.

———. *Letters of Mrs. Gaskell and Charles Eliot Norton 1855–1865*. Ed. Jane Whitehill. London: Oxford University Press, 1932.

Gissing, George. *London and the Life of Literature in Late Victorian England: The Diary of George Gissing, Novelist*. Ed. Pierre Coustillas. Hassocks, Sussex: Harvester Press, 1978.

Gladstone, William Ewart. *The Gladstone Diaries*. Ed. M. R. D. Foot. In progress. Oxford: Clarendon Press, 1968–.

Gray, Thomas. *Correspondence of Thomas Gray*. Ed. Paget Toynbee and Leonard Whibley. 3 vols. Oxford: Clarendon Press, 1935. Reprinted with corrections and additions by H. W. Starr, 1971.

Hardy, Thomas. *The Collected Letters of Thomas Hardy*. Ed. Richard Little Purdy and Michael Millgate. In progress. Oxford: Clarendon Press, 1978–.

Pepys, Samuel. *The Diary of Samuel Pepys*. Ed. Robert Latham and William Matthews. 11 vols. Berkeley: University of California Press, 1970–1983.

Tennyson, Alfred. *The Letters of Alfred Lord Tennyson*. Ed. Cecil Y. Lang and Edgar F. Shannon, Jr. In progress. Oxford: Clarendon Press, 1982–.

Tennyson, Emily. *The Letters of Emily Lady Tennyson*. Ed. James O. Hoge. University Park: Pennsylvania State University Press, 1974.

Thackeray, William Makepeace. *The Letters and Private Papers of William Makepeace Thackeray*. Ed. Gordon N. Ray. 4 vols. London: Oxford University Press, 1945–1946.

Turner, Thomas. *The Diary of Thomas Turner of East Hoathly, 1754–1765*. Ed. Florence Maria Turner. London: John Lane, 1925.

———. *The Diary of Thomas Turner, 1754–1765*. Ed. David Vaisey. Oxford: Clarendon Press, 1984.

———. *The Diary of a Georgian Shopkeeper*. Ed. G. H. Jennings. Oxford: Oxford University Press, 1979.

Voltaire. *Voltaire's Correspondence*. Ed. Theodore Besterman. 107 vols. Geneva: Institut et Musée Voltaire, 1953–1965.

Walpole, Horace. *Horace Walpole's Correspondence*. Yale Edition. Ed. W. S. Lewis. 48 vols. New Haven: Yale University Press, 1937–1983.

Wordsworth, Dorothy. *Journals of Dorothy Wordsworth*. Ed. Mary Moorman. London: Oxford University Press, 1971.

———. *Letters of Dorothy Wordsworth*. Sel. and ed. Alan G. Hill. Oxford: Oxford University Press, 1981.

Wordsworth, John. *The Letters of John Wordsworth*. Ed. Carl H. Ketcham. Ithaca: Cornell University Press, 1969.

Wordsworth, William. *Selected Letters of William Wordsworth*. Ed. Alan G. Hill. Oxford: Oxford University Press, 1984.

Wordsworth, William, and Dorothy. *The Letters of William and Dorothy Wordsworth*. Ed. Ernest de Selincourt. 6 vols. Oxford: Clarendon Press, 1935–1939. Rev. C. L. Shaver, Mary Moorman, Alan G. Hill. In progress. 1967–.

———. *The Love Letters of William and Mary Wordsworth*. Ed. Beth Darlington. London: Chatto and Windus, 1982.

Richard D. Altick

Bibliographies:
How Much Should
a Reviewer Tell?

The germs of this article can be found
in two reviews of bibliographical tools that purported to be of
use to scholars. One, appearing in the first volume (1979) of
Review, was an extremely critical analysis of a book forthrightly
entitled *Literary Research Guide: An Evaluative, Annotated Bibliography*. Never, as I suggested there, did so few words contain so
many questionable assertions. It was—and is—a book so laden
with misleading statements and sheer error that for fourteen
pages to be devoted to exposing shortcomings that any scholar
would detect at a glance seemed an act of overkill, like attacking a
flea with a sledgehammer. Yet the publisher had advertised the
book with samples of warm praise from half a dozen librarians'
journals. The quotes, it turned out, were perfectly fair represen-
tations of the respective reviewers' opinions. And for that reason, I decided to use the episode, like the present occasion, as an
opportunity to raise a few questions about quality control both in
literary bibliographies themselves and in reviews of those indispensable instruments of scholarship. The second germ lay in a
deservedly scathing review (*Literary Research Newsletter*, Summer 1980) of another book, *A Catalogue Checklist of English Prose
Fiction 1750–1800*. In his last paragraph, the reviewer raised a
point too seldom addressed in scholarly criticism, the publisher's
responsibility: "Any publisher honorably engaged in the production of academic books, especially nowadays," he wrote, "must
be willing to accept a burden of responsibility to enforce standards of excellence. Every person in the academic profession,
every reader and every author or aspiring author, has a right to

expect that publishers will assume that burden." Even the most scrupulous critics in the scholarly press cannot serve as the only guardians of standards. Quality control should be the concern of everybody involved in the gathering, evaluating, and disseminating of bibliographical information.

The fact is that the library press is too often an innocent but nonetheless culpable partner in the crime of encouraging shoddy bibliographies, even if its complicity consists only of standing by while incompetent bibliographers and complaisant publishers get away with it. In the current edition of the American librarians' bible, Sheehy's *Guide to Reference Books* (1976), two entries, among others, offend my eyes. One is the listing, without comment, of Chauncey Sanders's *Introduction to Research in English Literary History* (1952), which most readers of this document fortunately are too young to have known. It is so clumsy, indeed useless as a vade mecum for literary study, as to prompt one to reconsider one's principled scruples against book burning. The other Sheehy offense is the listing of Andrew Block's *The English Novel, 1740–1850: A Catalogue Including Prose Romances, Short Stories, and Translations of Foreign Fiction*, first published in 1939. Sheehy gives no hint that the *TLS* (1961) called this book "an alphabet of miscellaneous assertions, many of which are known to be inexact" and "the most cynically unbusinesslike document in the history of bibliography." Nor is mention made of Robert Colby's detailed review of the second, unchastened edition in *Nineteenth-Century Fiction* (1962).

Any scholar examining Sheehy or any of the other professional librarians' reference works designed to assist literary research of any kind must be oppressively conscious of the number of books listed, and thus inferentially recommended, which fail to pass even moderately stringent tests of accuracy and authority. In a lecture I delivered a decade ago at the Rutgers University Graduate School of Library Service—it has since had limited circulation as a pamphlet—I spoke of the way library shelves were booby-trapped with unauthoritative reference tools. "Many of them," I said, "are attractively packaged, giving every implicit indication that as many pains have been taken to ensure the purity of the contents as to enhance the format. But has this actually been the case? Unlike canned goods in an advanced state of ripeness, books give no outward sign of contamination." I therefore proposed that such books have a warning pasted on their spines: perhaps a scarlet *A* for adulteration. So far as I can determine, this excellent piece of free advice has never been acted on. This issue involves a tricky principle of librarianship: whether (to load the question) the public—the man or woman who comes off the street or the academic researcher—is better served by having all reference and bibliographical materials spread out in a vast cafeteria of truth and misinformation or by the librarians' own exercise of judgment guided by well-informed reviews of such tools in their professional journals.

My concern with the reliability of reviews in those journals, initially touched off by their blind praise of a wretched "literary research guide" that is even worse than Sanders's, is the more urgent because in the past half-dozen years the production of "scholarly" bibliographies of individual authors and literary genres has developed into a major branch of reference book publishing. Five firms specialize in these books: G. K. Hall in Boston, with its long series of Reference Publications in Literature; Gale in Detroit, with its Gale Information Guide Library; Garland in New York, with its Garland Reference Library of the Humanities; Scarecrow in Connecticut, with its Scarecrow Author Bibliographies; and Whitston in Troy, New York, the house that has brought us both the checklist of eighteenth-century fiction complained of above and the so-called New Sabin, a murky project which seems qualified to be an eighth type of ambiguity.

The sheer number of potentially valuable bibliographies this industry has turned out lately is, of course, a welcome development—at least in theory. As the bibliographical jungle grows thicker in inverse proportion to the way the Brazilian rain forests are being cleared, we need all the help we can get. But as yet, unless we perform our own close analysis of a volume whose contents are central to our own specialized interest, we have few dependable guides to the reliability of these books, many of which do not seem to have been reviewed at length in any journals. I would hope that before long we might have the advantage of a series of searching articles reviewing all the bibliographies published recently in each of the fields of English and American literary study.

Meanwhile, let me offer an example—I hope it will prove to be an extreme example of the genre, not a typical one—of the vulnerability of one such book, volume 12 in the Garland Reference Library of the Humanities: R. C. Churchill's *Bibliography of Dickensian Criticism 1836–1975* (1975). Perhaps because an earlier volume of the same general quality, William Miller's *The Dickens Student and Collector*, inspired what to my mind remains one of the classic rebukes of bibliographical incompetence, Philo Calhoun and Howell J. Heaney's "Dickensiana in the Rough" (*PBSA*, 1947), Dickens scholars have been especially sensitized to that brand of scholarly ineptitude. In any case, Churchill's book was mercilessly reviewed in, among other places, *The Dickensian* (1976), *The Library* (1977), the *Dickens Studies Newsletter* (1976) and the *Modern Language Review* (1977). Among other deficiencies and miscalculations, the reviewers singled out several for special mention. One was Churchill's vanity. Although he had no standing as a Dickens scholar or critic, his contributions being mainly limited to such effusions as a paper read to the Literary Society at Downing College, Cambridge, in 1937, he relentlessly quoted himself in annotations to the various items, his name thus accounting for the largest entry in the index. "The bibliography," said one reviewer, "is largely an autobiography, and if we are to judge from the frequency of entries, Mr. R. C. Churchill is the major critic of the whole period since 1836." Another charge related to the polemic tone, Dr. and Mrs. Leavis being the main, but by no means only, villains of Dickens criticism. "It is an uncommon man," wrote a second reviewer, "who would glimpse the possibility of conducting a vendetta in a bibliography; and Mr. Churchill is an uncommon bibliographer." Still another idiosyncrasy, to give it a kind name, was Churchill's devoting a disproportionate amount of attention to early twentieth-century criticism, a phase of Dickens commentary which most scholars agree was, with the exception of Chesterton and Gissing, one of the least provocative or enlightening. The bibliography was selective in two regrettable ways: Churchill "selected" as much congenial early twentieth-century criticism as he could find, and at the same time omitted hundreds of pertinent items, not least from the Victorian period despite the starting date of 1836. To attempt a list of omitted items, said the reviewer in the *Dickens Studies Annual,* "would fill more than the whole issue" in which this review appeared.

To give a full roster of what Dickens specialists found wrong with the book would likewise fill more than the whole space I allot myself for this article. But read what the reviewer in the *Library Journal* (1975) had to say: "Meticulously prepared and arranged, it is the most complete listing thus far published. Equal stress is placed on the Victorian, early twentieth-century and modern periods. Many of the citations are generously annotated with quotations from the work itself or from reviews. [The critic forbore to specify that Churchill was the principal reviewer quoted.] An indispensable guide." This contributor to the critical literature of the profession was a librarian in Natick, Massachusetts. She was a victim of, among other things, the widely observable human tendency to believe bibliographers' own puffs. Churchill maintained that his was "the most comprehensive [Dickens bibliography] yet attempted." Close readers may detect an escape clause in the last two words, but such modesty would seem inharmonious with the self-aggrandizement that marks the book as a whole. The Garland people certainly must have believed the claim. But it is unfortunate that they seem not to have asked the opinion of any responsible Dickens scholar, who might have rendered a quite different verdict.

The reception of Churchill's book was not made less ferocious by the accident that it appeared when two newly published Dickens bibliographies were available for instant comparison. One was the masterly section by Philip Collins in the third volume of the *New Cambridge Bibliography of English Literature*—a fitting supplement, as is also his updating in *Victorian Fiction: A Second Guide to Research* (1978), to Ada Nisbet's justly celebrated chapter in the first *Victorian Fiction* volume (1964). The other was Joseph Gold's *The Stature of Dickens: A Centenary Bibliography* (1971), to which, in my own view, both the specialists and the library reviewers were too well disposed. "Excellent," said *Choice* (whose notices of literary bibliographies, I should remark, are by and large the most discerning of a depressing lot). "Based on careful, extensive scholarship," said the *Library Journal* (1971). "It would be entirely wrong not to recognize its value and convenience." But a reviewer in *Nineteenth-Century Fiction* (1972) called attention to major flaws in the book's arrangement, the lack of cross-references, serious omissions, and downright errors.

Mention of Collins's admirable treatment of Dickens in the *NCBEL* III evokes a small irony that contains its own moral for our immediate purposes. The reviews of that volume included one in *Nineteenth-Century Fiction* (1971) in which the critic, using the Dickens section as the only sample examined in some detail, concluded on the basis of that one section that the whole volume was a success. The hazard involved in such lucky dipping is obvious. Actually, I do not think that reviewers, with two or three exceptions (*Victorian Studies*, 1971; *Journal of English and Germanic Philology*, 1971; the [British] *Library Review*, 1970) have done justice to that volume's weaknesses, and so, by extrapolation, to the deficiencies of the entire set. It is a more imperfect tool than it has any right to be. An editor accepting so huge a responsibility—the revision and supplementing of an already standard work—knew what he was getting into and was thus obligated to maintain the highest possible standard of bibliographical listing. One reason why the *NCBEL* falls signally short of that goal may lie in the meager set of instructions issued to the contributors. So large a collaborative enterprise cannot be conducted with a loose rein; there must be firm control from above. Permissiveness has no place in bibliography. As a consequence of this easygoing policy, the *NCBEL* is anything but what a brief paragraph in *PBSA*, of all places, deemed it to be (the judgment evidently resting on no more solid evidence than the jacket copy): "The bibliographical details of earlier editions," said the writer, "are collected and refined, and the work is fully up to date." Actually, the "bibliographical details" were far too often transferred to the new edition without "refinement," which presumably includes the systematic rechecking that would have revealed numerous errors; and even on the day it went to press the volume was not "fully up to date." None of the major reviews alluded to the most comprehensive enumeration of opportunities missed which was contained in a single paragraph of F. W. Bateson's letter to the *TLS* (25 December 1969), which indicated eight major ways in which the "standard *CBEL* information" might have been expanded in the entries for major authors' writings. These recommendations were part of Bateson's ill-tempered response to the fact that the volume was dedicated to him, the editor of the original edition, though he had long since washed his hands of the whole *NCBEL* project. After this cannonade, any subsequent reviews inevitably seemed like fusillades of buckshot. In any event, it appears to me that the *NCBEL* by and large is venerated less reservedly than it should be.

What criteria should reviewers apply to bibliographies? Whether they write for their fellow scholars or for their fellow librarians, the standards must be the same, for their dedication to truth in humane learning is the same, whether they serve scholars or the celebrated, but never satisfactorily defined, "general public." The bookseller P. H. Muir once reviewed a compilation called *Victorian Detective Fiction*, the unelaborated catalogue of a private collection of which Graham Greene was half owner. The earlier reviews, all unflattering, had illustrated two contrasting ways of damning a bibliography. The *TLS* reviewer (1966), shirking his professional obligation to come down to brass tacks, had merely pointed out that neither of the adjectives in the title was accurate and then, faithful to the hallowed *TLS* tradition of killing a book with a quip, demanded, "Why, in the categories entered in the Index of Detectives, has Dogs been omitted?" In *The Book Collector*, David Randall, no less severe but more specific, had summed up the book as "a curious smorgasbord" of "an amateur's collection" and uttered a rather more pertinent query of his own: "Why, one wonders, was it ever produced?" In *The Library* (1968) Muir, equally dismissive, concluded by laying down the two criteria which, for him, distinguished amateurism from professionalism: "Book-collecting . . . is idiosyncratic and selective, whereas bibliography is authoritative and inclusive." We can begin by adopting these two requirements, authority and inclusiveness, as indispensable.

Above all, the authoritative bibliography is one whose information is based on first-hand knowledge of every item cited. It distrusts every predecessor, including previous editions of itself. When judged by this standard, the *NCBEL* falls short. This point need not be discussed further. Every one of us has favorite examples of untrustworthy, nonauthoritative bibliographies on which, if they have not, unhappily, been superseded, he vents periodic maledictions.

Inclusiveness is a test which, I fear, most of the recent crop of Hall-Gale-Garland-Scarecrow, etc. bibliographies fail. One such is Robert B. White's Gale publication, *The English Literary Journal to 1900.* The *Library Journal* reviewer (1977) found nothing wrong with it except that "the compiler has a love affair with *Notes and Queries*, which is practically indexed here" (overlooking the fact that a great deal of out-of-the-way information on such a subject is found nowhere else but in *N&Q*). *Choice* (1978) called it "valuable"; no criticism offered. But the *TLS* reviewer (1977) complained, as he well might have done, of the early cutoff date—1972; he pointed out, again with good reason, that the terminus a quo, 1890, entailed the omission of references to much useful earlier material; along with others, he deemed the coverage of the eighteenth century superior to that of the nineteenth, as befitted a student of Richmond P. Bond (but of course that did not extenuate the lighter coverage of a considerably more important phase of the topic); and, not incidentally, he regretted the compiler's failure to define what "a literary journal" was. The reviewer in *The Library* (1977) called attention to the many literary journals, properly so called, which were omitted—and to a Columbia dissertation of 1965 which had given the subject much fuller treatment.

This last point is particularly apropos here. However well intentioned and earnestly prepared, the Hall–Gale–Garland-, etc. bibliographies are commissioned by commercial publishers who impose space limitations and deadlines on their authors. They do not encourage inclusiveness, which would prolong the term of preparation almost indefinitely as well as expand the book to an unprofitable size. Bibliographies that make a legitimate claim to exhaustiveness (which I take it is one degree short of completeness, an unachievable goal) require more time than most bibliographers under contract to a commercial publisher have at their command. Dissertation writers dedicated to covering the same field have, under ideal conditions, such as the implacable zeal for perfection harbored by some doctoral advisers, a better claim to scholarly respect. But the Hall–Gale, etc. books usually preempt their various fields, making it far less likely that a superior job will find a publisher. This is one realm of publishing where competition is not desired. If a proffered bibliographical manuscript has been anticipated by someone else's publication, and if the publisher to whom it has been submitted knows this, that's it. There are few Maecenases who will risk producing a fresh bibliography of Joseph Crabtree, "that ridiculously neglected poet of the eighteenth century," no matter how superior it is to the existing one, if libraries' budgets do not allow for what would appear to be sheer duplication. Under present and foreseeable conditions, Macbeth's wisdom, slightly emended, is unarguable: "If it were done at all, 'twere well/It were done right in the first place."

There remain, besides authority and inclusiveness, two further requirements: accuracy (which is not identical with authority, but a subdivision) and ease of use. Nothing wastes a scholar's time as often and as needlessly as a bibliography that cannot be trusted in the all-important small details. A compiler may conform religiously to the first requirement, that he establish the existence and nature of each item by first-hand examination, but he labors to little effect if he allows errors to creep either into his original transcription of the bibliographical information or into its eventual printed form. In my own experience, the worst offender has been the annual Victorian bibliography in *Victorian Studies*. The decennial cumulation for 1965–74, published in offset form by another firm that is achieving prominence in the scholarly and bibliographical line, the AMS Press of New York, perpetuates an inadmissible number of inconsistencies and typos. One can charitably attribute to the compositor errors that actually were in the contributor's or editor's copy prepared for the annual edition, but realism insists that the buck stop not at the printer's but at the editorial office where somebody reads the proofs.

On one page of this volume, to cite a single instance out of far too many that present themselves, I found myself credited with an article in *PBSA*, in such-and-such a volume at such-and-such pages. I had indeed written an article with the title given, and it had appeared in a volume with that number and on the pages so meticulously specified. The only catch was that it was a volume of *Studies in Bibliography*, not *PBSA*. Who was to know that the wrong journal was cited? This particular kind of gaffe is not included in the three and half pages of Errata, which are "Limited to proper names and selected titles to prevent misreading; first names are corrected in the index." Some 160 errors of only the kind specified are a rather impressive number for any one volume of a bibliography. But if it had been possible to correct the pages of the original issues from which the collected volume was photographically offset, I could have supplied several times as many from my deplorably marked-up personal copies, including the misadventure of my own article. And no matter if the errata list was almost exhaustive; what good would it do? I suspect that few of us, using such a tool, systematically look in the back to see if some error has been noted in the information we are concerned with.

What might be termed the old style of inconvenience in bibliographies is illustrated by the *NCBEL* practice of listing secondary material chronologically, or rather quasi-chronologically— all the books and articles by a single critic being appended to his first entry. The new style of inconvenience is occasioned by the necessary employment of "key words" in computerized bibliographies, which makes the use of Lawrence McNamee's bibliography of dissertations in English and American literature much more complicated than it should be, and, I should add, more conducive to accidental oversight. But even McNamee's system of code numbers and cross-references is acceptable when compared with the tyranny of the key word in *Dissertation Abstracts*, where Lewis Carroll and Lewis Mumford are interfiled, as librarians say, with Sinclair Lewis, Wyndham Lewis, C. Day Lewis, C. S. Lewis, and Matthew G. Lewis; and where O. Henry rubs shoulders, uneasily one would think, with Henry James. And may whatever gods preside over scholarly endeavor guide the reference-seeker to the hiding places of dissertations whose fancy titles don't contain any proper names that could be converted into key words. One sometimes yearns for the improbable day when it is realized that the undoubted practical advantages of computerized bibliography have meant sacrificing certain ones attainable only by the manual intelligence, so to speak, of the human being. Meanwhile, it is only by constant complaint—of which this is a tentative model—that computer scientists will be pushed to devise ways by which their machines can enhance, not diminish, the ease of bibliographical search.

Which neatly leads into the peroration. If standards of bibliographical records are to be maintained, let alone raised, they require the cooperation of all interested parties. Back in 1956, Lionel Trilling wrote for *The Griffin*, the organ of the Readers' Subscription Club, a piece called "The Farmer and the Cowboy Make Friends." I would be willing to make a small bet that that essay happens not to be recorded in the standard annual bibliographies and that therefore nobody knows about it except through expertise in the Trilling canon. But that is not the point, nor does the subject of the essay bear on the present one. I merely suggest that somehow the farmers and the cowboys into whose respective classes the reviewers of bibliographical works are divided—the scholarly ones and the contributors to the library press—must not only make friends but informally cooperate. Given a reasonably high standard of bibliographical acceptability among the scholarly reviewers, I should like to see reviewers in the library press routinely reading and absorbing the judgments of the scholarly press, so that they could bear in mind, and even convey to their clientele, the wholesome warning that certain surgeon generals of bibliographical scholarship have determined that this or that new volume is dangerous to your—if not health, then your apprehension of truth, which I suppose *is* a kind of mental health.

If the reviewers for library periodicals, as well as the writers of standard guides to reference books, would be more stringent in their standards, offering in effect a continuing series of consumer reports, they might reduce the market for shoddy bibliographical products. I imagine that sooner or later the publishers would get the message and institute some form of quality control, most desirably seeking and acting on the advice of accredited scholars who could dissuade them from undertaking travesties like the two books I mentioned at the beginning.

No doubt the measures I propose are a little divorced from reality. Academic reviewers come in various grades of quality, including the stern and the softhearted, and not all of them can be expected to declare of a peccant bibliographer, "This will never do." Librarians cannot easily be persuaded to keep abreast of pertinent scholarly literature, and even less to allow their professional judgments to be swayed by what they read in a field wrongly assumed to be alien to their own. Publishers will be loath to let the unpractical habitués of the ivory tower (an apocryphal structure still widely believed in) complicate their commercial lives. But we are all scholars, and scholars are, almost by definition, hospitable to counsels of perfection.

Note

A version of this essay was first presented to the Midwest Modern Language Association in 1981.

James L. W. West III

Descriptive Bibliography, Detective Fiction, and Knowing the Rules

Of the various genres and subgenres of literary scholarship, surely descriptive bibliography is the least well understood and, year in and year out, is the most ineptly reviewed. Often the reviewer is recruited only because he has "written something" on the author treated in the bibliography. The reviewer begins by wanting to do a competent job, but confronted with descriptive formularies, gutter measurements, and offset slur, he quickly concludes that he is about as well equipped to review a full-dress bibliography as he is to assess a volume on particle physics. He responds with vague praise and puffery, makes some comments about how useful everyone is going to find this book, mails in the review, shelves the bibliography, and probably never opens it again.

This is ironic, because descriptive bibliographies are not difficult to review, or to use. They are the very devil to compile, of course, but if one does the work correctly, he produces a research tool that is relatively simple for other scholars to make use of. A descriptive bibliography is no more and no less than a formulaic description, in ideal terms, of a group of literary artifacts. From the descriptions and notes the scholar can deduce important things about an author's career, or about several books on the same subject, or about several editions of the same work, or about a period in literary history. Descriptive bibliographies can be used in much the same ways that biographies and historical surveys are used, and the marks of high quality are the same in all three kinds of scholarship. A poor descriptive bibliography is a fragmented, inaccurate mass of data that presents finally no integrated or comprehensible picture of its subject. A good descriptive bibliography, by contrast, is a unified and reliable statement about a work or period or genre, or, alternately, is a coherent and usable account of an author's professional career.

But what about the rules and strictures? Must the reviewer master the arcane formularies and elaborate symbols set forth in Fredson Bowers's *Principles of Bibliographical Description* (1949) and in G. Thomas Tanselle's various articles on descriptive bibliography? Isn't the genre finally so dependent on specialized knowledge that only an initiate can review competently an example of it? The answer is that the formularies used by descriptive bibliographers are not especially complicated or hard to learn, and the practices that they follow vary widely. The recommendations of Bowers and Tanselle are not rigid; every bibliographer finds instances in which he must depart from them. Sometimes he must even invent his own approaches when he discovers printing practices or types of data not anticipated by Bowers, Tanselle, or any of the other theorists.

With regard to rules, and the bending or breaking of them, it might be said that descriptive bibliography resembles detective fiction. There are certain regulations that the compiler of a descriptive bibliography, like the author of a puzzle mystery, must follow. Monsignor Ronald A. Knox, in his *Ten Commandments of Detection* (1929), stipulated among other things that the criminal must be mentioned early in the story, that the reader must not be allowed to follow the criminal's thoughts, and that supernatural or preternatural agencies must not figure in the solution. Monsignor Knox further insisted that the detective must not solve the murder through an unaccountable intuition, that he must not himself commit the crime, and that all information available to him must also be presented to the reader.

The author of a traditional whodunit must follow these rules, but there are other conventions from which he can stray. The sidekick, the Watson, does not have to narrate, for example, and he can vary enormously in personality and function from mystery to mystery. Indeed there does not have to be a Watson, nor does the author have to include the customary "assembly" in the penultimate chapter—the scene in which all of the suspects gather in one room and the detective proceeds, by questioning and logic, to unmask the culprit. Other rules are even weaker. Sherlock Holmes to the contrary, there *can* be a love interest in a detective yarn. There can even be political, historical, or social themes, providing the author does not pursue them too insistently.

Genius reveals itself most fully, said Goethe, when it works within limitations. Great poets, according to many critics, show their talents best when composing within fairly rigid verse forms—traditional ones like the sonnet or villanelle, or forms of their own devising. The best works of detective fiction come about when accomplished practitioners of the genre experiment within the boundaries of the form. Likewise, excellent descriptive bibliographies are compiled by energetic, skilled bibliographers working imaginatively within their scholarly genre, not by poorly informed bibliographers cutting corners or breaking rules needlessly.

The reviewer of a descriptive bibliography, like the student of the puzzle mystery, should therefore acquaint himself with (1) those things the author *must* do and always does; (2) those things he *should* do and usually does; and (3) those things he *could* do but often does not do. In the first category, the mandatory one, the reviewer should require that the bibliographer quasi-facsimile all title pages, and probably all copyright and dedication pages as well, and that he provide paragraphs for collation, contents, running titles, binding or casing, and jacket or wrappers. The bibliographer should also present paragraphs on typography and paper (though many bibliographers do not), and there ought to be a record of copies examined, unless the bibliography is based on a single collection or group of three or four collections. A descriptive bibliographer must attempt to give dates of publication for all major books; he should also give printing runs for editions and impressions if he can.

The reviewer should require that the terminology be consistent. If a particular decoration is called a "rule" on p. 175, a "border" on p. 193, and an "ornament" on p. 254, then the bibliographer has not been paying attention. The format of entries must be consistent as well, with information presented in the same order from entry to entry. If note 1 in entry A1a gives the date of publication, the retail price, and the printing run of the first impression, then all subsequent note 1's ought to give this information, unless, of course, the bibliographer has been unable to secure it. In such a case, note 1 must say that the data were unavailable.

The bibliographer ought to use his introduction as more than an occasion to thank librarians, collectors, and bookdealers. In his prefatory matter he needs to align himself with those biblio-graphical theorists he proposes to follow, explain why he has chosen not to follow other theorists, and state his alternate intentions. He must make clear his stance on *issue* and *state*, say what organizing principle he proposes to use (alphabetical, chronological, or some combination of the two), explain his numbering system, and comment on his indexing principles. He must also tell the reader what insights he has derived from his work. If his data have revealed important information about printing practices in eighteenth-century London, then what ex-actly have they revealed? If his formularies and notes tell us new things about an author's professional career, or about his rela-tionships with his publishers, or about his compositional habits, then what precisely do they tell us? Bibliographical information almost never speaks for itself, not even to the initiated. The bibliographer is obligated to reveal what he has found, in straightforward prose.

The reviewer should check whether the bibliographer has differentiated between and among his "B" items. The B section in a bibliography is invariably troublesome. It contains "Contri-butions to Books," a heading so vague that it can cover a great many kinds of publications. There are three major kinds of items that end up in B sections: true contributions to books—writings executed for inclusion in particular volumes and published for the first time there; first book appearances—republications (usu-ally in collections by divers hands) of items that have appeared in print elsewhere, often in periodicals or newspapers; and anthology reprints—publications identical to first book appearances except that they lack the element of "firstness." These classes of items are like apples, oranges, and tangerines. All are fruit, but the second two resemble each another more than either resembles the first. The bibliographer must show that he is aware of these distinctions and must make them carefully in his listings.

There are various practices a bibliographer *should* follow, and almost always does follow. If he has not done so, the reviewer may legitimately fault him. The bibliographer, for example, should investigate the history of his author's works in transatlantic editions—British editions for an American author, American editions for a British author. Here the bibliographer should be careful to specify whether he is tracing the publishing history of the work of art or the printing history of the image of the text. Modern photo-offset technology has made it common for the publishing history of an author's English editions to be intertwined with that of his American editions. Probably it is best, in such cases, to separate the two lines of publication in vertical listings and show the interrelationships in a stemma.

There should be illustrations in a descriptive bibliography; even the most niggardly publisher will allow a few line cuts or halftones. The reviewer should decide whether these illustrations are functional or merely decorative. Are the images sharp? Are the exemplars in good condition? I recall several illustrations in one of the bibliographies in the Pittsburgh Series for which the glassine wrappers had not been removed when photographs were taken of the dust jackets. The halftones, as a result, were marred by reflections of the photographer's flash attachment. And certain very common dust jackets reproduced in one of the Pittsburgh volumes looked like Maggie's drawers (tattered and torn). Purchasers of these descriptive bibliographies should have been better served.

Bibliographers should include negative or inconclusive evidence in a full-dress compilation, but many do not, either because such evidence is hard to present gracefully or because the bibliographer does not wish to admit that he has invested time and come up with nothing. He thinks of the questions he often hears from outsiders: "What if you do the collations and discover no variants? Or measure the gutters and find no concealed printings? Or compare all of the endpapers and find them identical? Haven't you wasted your time?" The answer is that if the bibliographer has performed the labor, he should leave a record of it. If his author or his subject is important enough, then there will be a subsequent bibliographer who will need to know what worked and what did not.

Bibliographers should investigate an author's published and unpublished correspondence for clues about his texts. I recall my puzzlement ten years ago when I prepared an entry for the first French edition of William Styron's *Lie Down in Darkness* and noticed that the heroine's name had been changed from *Peyton* in the American text to *Marjorie* in the French. I had no notion why the Paris publisher should have made the change; I dutifully mentioned it in a note and passed on. Had I read through Styron's correspondence with his father from this period, then already available at Duke University Library, I would have come upon a letter in which Styron explained the change. The publisher had made the alteration, wrote young Styron with some delicacy, because *Peyton* sounds like the French word for the rumblings one's stomach makes after a large meal. Styron might have added that *pet* is French slang for "fart," and that *-ton* is a common diminutive ending.

There are several kinds of work that descriptive bibliographers *could* perform but usually do not. Reviewers should not be too severe in their criticisms if bibliographers have avoided these areas; they should be generous in their praise if bibliographers have investigated them. The subject most frequently neglected by descriptive bibliographers, especially by those who compile single-author volumes, is publishing history. A single-author listing is primarily a record of a writer's literary career, but it is also a partial account of the business practices of the author's publishers. If there are histories of these publishing firms or memoirs written by the heads of the houses, then the bibliographer should have read them. He should take care to relate his data, by allusion and documentation, to the stories of the publishing houses. The bibliographer should also be knowledgeable about the history of the publishing industry during the author's productive years. Were the practices of Publisher X typical for the times? Was Publisher Y flush, or was he operating on a shoestring? Was the author's masterpiece issued during a slow season, or was the competition stiff that spring? Such information injects life and relevance into otherwise inert data.

Hand collations from edition to edition and machine collations within editions are useful, but the reviewer should remember that a descriptive bibliography is not necessarily a collection of materials for a scholarly edition. If such collations have been performed, well and good; the reviewer should check the lists for accuracy. If they have not been done, the reviewer should only note this fact in a neutral way.

A good friend at another university maintains that by the time most members of our profession have been out of graduate school for ten years, they have become ineducable. Their research interests have become so specialized and their critical thinking so firmly set that they are incapable of assimilating new information or of learning new skills. I hope that my friend is wrong. Specifically I hope that in the future more reviewers of descriptive bibliographies will be willing to school themselves in the rudiments of the discipline. The rules that govern the making of descriptive bibliographies are not a great deal more elaborate or rigid than those that govern the writing of murder mysteries. The reviewer must simply take time to acquaint himself with these rules before he attempts to comment intelligently on the genre.

Readings for Prospective Reviewers of Descriptive Bibliographies

Abbott, Craig S. "A System of Bibliographical Reference Numbering." *PBSA* 69 (1975):67–74.
———. "Offset Slur as Bibliographical Evidence." *PBSA* 70 (1976):538–41.
Bowers, Fredson. *Principles of Bibliographical Description.* Princeton: Princeton Univ. Press, 1949.

————. *Essays in Bibliography, Text, and Editing.* Charlottesville: Published for the Bibliographical Society of the University of Virginia by the Univ. Press of Virginia, 1975.

Jones, John Bush, ed. *Readings in Descriptive Bibliography.* Kent, Ohio: Kent State Univ. Press, 1974. Contains a useful checklist (pp. 206–8) of further readings on descriptive bibliography.

Shillingsburg, Peter L. "Detecting the Use of Stereotype Plates." *Editorial Quarterly* 1 (1975):2–3.

————. "Register Measurement as a Method of Detecting Hidden Printings." *PBSA* 73 (1979):484–88.

Tanselle, G. Thomas. *Selected Studies in Bibliography.* Charlottesville: Published for the Bibliographical Society of the University of Virginia by the Univ. Press of Virginia, 1979.

————. "The Identification of Type Faces in Bibliographical Description." *PBSA* 60 (1966):185–202.

————. "The Descriptive Bibliography of American Authors." *Studies in Bibliography* 21 (1968):1–24.

————. "Book-Jackets, Blurbs, and Bibliographers." *The Library,* 5th ser., 26 (1971):91–134.

————. "The Bibliographical Concepts of *Issue* and *State.*" *PBSA* 69 (1975):17–66.

West, James L. W., III. "The Bibliographical Concept of *Plating.*" *Studies in Bibliography* 36 (1983):252–66.

————. " 'Section B' and the Bibliographer." *Analytical & Enumerative Bibliography* 7 (1983):31–36.

Robert L. Patten

Reviewing Reviewing:
From the Editor's Desk

> *Book reviews . . . [generate] far more pas-*
> *sion than sex does in the literary world.*
>
> THOMAS FLEMING

Reviews serve different purposes at different times and for different constituencies. In an editor's view, as contrasted to an author's or a publisher's, there are therefore many different kinds of good reviews. Two recent taxonomies of reviews illustrate how categories and evaluations of reviews depend on the bias of a particular constituency. Wayne Booth, speaking from the author's viewpoint, lists "three criteria for good reviews": (1) to give the ready-made reader an accurate report and a clear appraisal; (2) to entice the indifferent or hostile reader into the enterprise; and (3) to advance the inquiry by vexing the author (and others) into thought.[1] These are purposes legitimized by the author, who wants the reader to understand correctly what the book says, who wants buyers, and if the book's thesis is going to be challenged, wants that challenge to be thought-provoking.

Herbert Lindenberger, looking at the same subject from a slightly different angle, subdivides "the genre of reviews into its characteristic forms": (1) the all-outer (positive or negative), notable for its totality of response; (2) the niggler (also positive or negative), which refuses to generalize about the book, but concentrates instead on details; (3) the displacer, in which the work becomes a springboard for the reviewer's own ideas or own notion of how the study ought to have been conducted; and (4) the summarizer, which restates the book's main points, often gleaned from the introduction, chapter titles, and "whatever generalizations catch the reviewer's eye."[2] Lindenberger's terms indicate that his sympathy, as an author who had undergone reviews—an experience about as enjoyable as going to the dentist, and as uncertain of outcome—is with the first of the four forms. And yet, as an editor, I can imagine circumstances in which I would commission any of them.

I

Practitioners of Reviewmanship recognize that the primary purpose of reviewing a book is to display one's talents, punish an enemy or achieve power.

RICHARD LINGEMAN

Maintaining that reviews serve many functions, while conceding that "Reviewmanship" must be minimized, is the first contribution an editor can make to this discussion. Reviews can sell books (or kill the sale), can sell the reviewing journal (always an important consideration for the journal's managers), can establish or destroy an author's reputation or a reviewer's, can do a combination of these things, or do none of them. Reviews can even be, on rare occasions, essays that delight in their own right, not simply pedestrian glosses on an absent text.

Academic monographs are mainly purchased by libraries. The reviews that most often influence collection-development librarians are those appearing in the *Kirkus Review*, which prints prepublication-date reviews to meet the needs of libraries whose collection-development policies require a book to have been reviewed before a purchase order may be written, and in *Choice*, the *Library Journal*, *Publishers Weekly*, and the *Wilson Library Bulletin*. These notices, written by librarians and teachers and usually but not always attributed, are succinct and summary in judgment. They sometimes identify the subgroup most likely to use the book (undergraduates, graduates, faculty, general public). And while they have little prestige among the professoriat, they probably sell the majority of copies of specialist academic monographs, be they on fiscal policy during the Directorate or Dravidian kinship terminologies in South India, on Chinese funerary sculpture or sexual identity in the plays of Christopher Marlowe. These notices combine aspects of Booth's first category ("an accurate report and a clear appraisal") with Lindenberger's fourth ("the summarizer"). But though they may be effective in the marketplace, they are seldom cited by publishers in their blurbs, by authors or reviewers in their vitas, or by historians in their retrospectives of scholarship.

A high percentage of scholarly monographs seldom get any other kind of evaluation. American university presses are moderately aggressive about promoting their titles and cautiously generous about distributing review copies to respected journals. But monographs that are issued as one in a series by domestic educational institutions (for example, the Duquesne [University] Studies, Language and Literature Series, or Penn State's SCN [Seventeenth-Century News] Editions and Studies), their affiliates (for example, the occasional papers published by the Williams Andrews Clark Memorial Library, of UCLA), and foreign titles from whatever source—university press, commercial publisher, or the egregious Salzburg Studies—are likely to go unnoticed. Foreign publishers are especially niggardly about sending review copies, at least to the United States; and American university presses have not been particularly effective in promoting and distributing their books abroad. Joint publication between two national publishing houses sometimes helps, but academic books still have trouble crossing national frontiers. And works in a series often slip by unremarked in advertising and promotion. So two further observations I would offer from the perspective of the editor's desk are first, that not all deserving books get reviewed—through no fault of the author though perhaps some fault of the publisher and distributor—and second, that the reviews many books do get appear in places that may sell copies to university, college, and public libraries but do not enhance the author's scholarly reputation or reach specialists in the field.

The journal which probably covers more kinds of books, and more books, than any other, and which gives those books reviews the academic community would recognize as scholarly, is the *TLS*. It tries to notice not just works with wide popular appeal, like biographies, but also highly specialized studies and potential best sellers such as dictionaries and anthologies that rarely get attention elsewhere. To be noticed in the *TLS* at all is an honor, and for many, the amount of space devoted to a book, even more than what is said in that space, is the index to the book's significance. A full page of fulminations about Christopher Hill's latest revisionary views on Puritanism probably does more for Hill's reputation (and sales) than a column inch of unstinted praise does for *X*'s first novel, though that column inch may with luck come to the attention of prize committees.

Since the *TLS* has gone over to the policy of identifying reviewers, the journal no longer speaks with anonymous and consequently magisterial authority; it is more a polyphonic forum, though insiders maintain that editorial biases can be detected. (Anti-Americanism, antistructuralism, and antifeminism are some of the broader categories of bias alleged.) Perhaps, but in all publications that work against stringent deadlines, inadvertence is as much a factor as editorial maneuvering. Review copies don't arrive, or are lost on the way to the reviewer; reviewers don't turn in copy on time, don't turn in the right amount of copy, don't turn it in at all; a long review bumps a short notice, which then gets lost in the shuffle; or several medium-sized reviews slip ahead of a long piece, which gradually loses its timeliness as it sits on the shelf. What looks like deliberation or even malice to the suffering author turns out to be accident. From the editor's desk, further maxims: one cannot assume that the absence of a review means that the journal or editor or reviewer hated the book, or ignored it. And for certain journals, of which the *TLS* and the *New York Times Book Review* are representative, any review, no matter how scathing, may be better than none at all.

There are journals with the prestige, and the quality of audience, that the *TLS* and the *New York Times* command, but with more restricted focus. The *New York Review of Books* and the *London Review of Books* offer the closest contemporary version of the great nineteenth-century quarterlies: long and often politically conscious critiques that aspire to an imperial cognition. Not to be reviewed in them is not, in most cases, to be slighted. Few books are chosen, and those that are, ranging the gamut from political science to interpretive theory and from the graphic arts to pop culture, appeal to an international intellectual elite largely of the left rather than the right. Earnest works by aspiring specialists rarely make the grade.

These journals encourage kinds of reviews that Booth might validate as "vexing the author . . . into thought," but that Lindenberger might well stigmatize as using "the work as a springboard for the reviewer's own ideas or own notion of how the study ought to have been conducted." When Harold Bloom begins a review of two new editions of Edgar Allan Poe's works with the words "Valéry, in a letter to Gide," the reader knows immediately that what follows will be a characteristic Bloomian meditation: high-class literary gossip under the guise of misprision ("the continued French overvaluation of Poe as lyrist"), reviewer's conundrums inflated to interpretive crises ("Poe's survival raises perpetually the issue whether literary merit and canonical status necessarily go together"), synopsis by rhetorical figure ("Poe's trope is 'absorption' "), and global comparison ("Poe's mythology, like the mythology of psychoanalysis . . . is peculiarly appropriate to any modernism").[3] If the Library of America Poe editors, Patrick F. Quinn and G. R. Thompson, want an assessment of their editorial skills and decisions, they need to go elsewhere—to the *PBSA* or *Studies in Bibliography* or *American Literature*. Bloom announces at the beginning that he's doing something else: using the occasion of the publication of a new selective edition of Poe's works in a format intended for widespread national circulation to evaluate Poe's contribution to nineteenth-century American poetry. And that turns out to be meager: according to Bloom, "Poe scrambles for twelfth place with Sidney Lanier."

Purists may reprobate such a review, but to reiterate my thesis, there are many legitimate reasons for writing and for reading reviews, and surely Bloom's assessment of Poe's achievement is one. Many will disagree with the conclusion he reaches, but as editor I could defend his decision to treat the publication of these texts not in terms of comprehensiveness of canon or bibliographic accuracy but in terms of Poe's importance. Especially because the reviewer is himself such an important and original critic, now turning his attention to the writers of the American Renaissance.

The Bloom example can stand as one instance of the review more significant for the reviewer than for the work reviewed. Authors—Lindenberger is one of them—may hate such indulgences of the reviewer's ego, but posterity often preserves these essays while more modest and circumspect reviewers disappear. Henry James may have been unfair to Dickens, Thackeray, and Trollope in his early days as a reviewer, but he was razing ground before erecting on the site his own house of fiction, and his reviews are now read less as judgments on his fellow novelists than as provisional formulations of his own theories. Similarly, no one cares any longer about the silly novels by lady novelists that George Eliot reviewed, but her pronouncements on the responsibilities of fiction are still important, for assessing her own work and for measuring subsequent achievements as well. When Joyce Carol Oates reviews a volume of poems in the *New York Times Book Review*, or John Updike tackles some work of belles lettres in the *New Yorker*, we are treated to a working author's version of what makes sense in the world, and such reviews may need to be judged less on how objectively they treat the work under discussion than on how they use that work in the elucidation of their own vision. Samuel Johnson, Samuel Taylor Coleridge, Matthew Arnold, Algernon Charles Swinburne, T. S. Eliot, Virginia Woolf, V. S. Pritchett—the English tradition is particularly rich in examples of writer-reviewers, whereas in the United States the two activities may have been kept more separate, with such figures as Edmund Wilson and Lionel Trilling bridging the gap. Thus even Lindenberger's "displacer" has a place in the editor's scheme of things.

When most academic authors talk about reviews, however, they mean those in the prestigious professional journals. These can take anywhere from a year to four years or more to appear. Such delays ensure that the notices are unhelpful to publishers trying to unload stock—no doubt more than one author has received a strongly favorable notice after the book has been remaindered. Instead, such evaluations have become an important contribution to tenure decisions, to other kinds of promotion, and more vaguely but also more pervasively to the scholar's reputation. If these kinds of scholarly assessments are likely to be the most thorough, informed, and judicious, they are also, potentially at least, the most contaminated by extraneous considerations. Many of those competent to judge a work know the author, since communities of specialists are small in number; some of those have fundamental ideological or theoretical disagreements with the work's assumptions; others may have reviewed earlier versions as colleagues or readers for the press; others have already been commissioned by another journal, or are busy or on leave or don't do reviews or got such bad notices on their last work that editors are reluctant to commission anything from them.

And since an author's whole professional life may hang in the balance, modern reviewers shy away from the "all-outer" (negative variety), preferring a judicious blend of favorable and unfavorable comment. (Lindenberger admits in a 1980 postscript to his essay that before launching into his first negative all-outer he "made sure the author was of tenure-level rank and thus cleared myself of any possible guilt for helping kick still another young academic out on the street!")[4] Even A. E. Housman might have moderated his devastating acerbity in the face of the present job market for classicists. It takes a great deal of courage and conviction and research to mount a full-scale attack on a scholarly book. Indeed, there is something of a law of the inverse that operates in these reviews: blander and kinder assessments are often made of weak works, while those that can sustain intellectual challenge are subjected to a drubbing.

Another factor affecting the quality of academic reviewing is time. Few scholars spend on a review a fraction of the time they spend in writing their own scholarly and critical articles. Many professional vitas do not enumerate reviews, but simply lump them together in this fashion: "Reviews in *Milton Studies, Philological Quarterly,* and *Shakespeare Studies.*" Since reviewing is not widely considered to be a mode of advancement within the profession, it is relegated to last place in the scholar's priorities, and the book under examination often receives only a cursory examination. A summarizer can learn to get by with a quick skim of the table of contents, the preface, and the first and last chapters, and if those portions are sampled fairly and paraphrased accurately, the resulting review may at least meet Booth's first criterion: "To give the ready-made reader an accurate report and a clear appraisal." That the journal of the professional association of teachers of language and literature, *PMLA*, does not print reviews, signals the secondary place reviewing takes in the minds of most of its members.

Seldom is adequate space assigned for a quality review. What can one say that might go to the heart of a work's conception and execution, and to its place in the history of criticism or scholarship, in three hundred to five hundred words? And how can an editor know which books, in the hands of which reviewers, deserve more room, especially when per-page costs run so high, so many books clamor for attention, and most readers consult the articles rather than the reviews in the first place? To big-name authors, and big-name reviewers, editors sometimes allocate more space; but on the whole, economic as well as time and prestige constraints operate against substantial reviews of important scholarly monographs by informed scholars who have not achieved international celebrity.

Review articles, and the journal *Review*, have tried to solve this problem;[5] but while writing about six or eight books in two thousand words may allow the reviewer more opportunity to establish the context of the works under examination, the actual word count per work may not be significantly higher. And unfortunately, with rare exceptions, these articles are not widely read or cited. Essays that survey the year's work are increasingly popular, but the judgments contained within them are usually terse and often subject to the overt biases imposed by the reviewer's chosen method of organizing the multiplicity of materials, and by implicit biases of temperament, training, and philosophy. For instance, there has been something of a running battle among *Studies in English Literature* reviewers between those who believe that editions are the publications of most significance and those who prefer works of criticism or theory within the field. By the luck of the draw, the editor of any particular year's edition of Dickens's novels or Mill's letters may legitimately feel slighted, while in another year it is the author advancing a new theory of reading or challenging the prevailing view of Shelley's Neoplatonic imagery who feels aggrieved. Balance among the reviewers' biases over time does nothing to right the balance in any one year's work.

Sometimes the most informed and careful reviews appear in the most specialized publications, the newsletters and quarterlies of the societies devoted to the study of a single author or subject. Newly minted Ph.D.s may possess a familiarity with the details of a topic that their senior colleagues have forgotten, may be more receptive to innovative approaches, and may devote more time and energy to these early efforts at reviewing than will be available to them at later stages of their careers. Their judgments are likely to be less trammeled by the conflicts arising out of acquaintance with the author, and perhaps to be more pointed, as they too compete for tenure and promotion. On the other side of the ledger, their perspective may still be narrow, their partisanship may be untempered by time, their experience of writing a thesis may incline them to niggle about relatively insignificant flaws, and their capacity to shape the review itself into an artful essay may still be quite limited. And there is always the possibility that the younger scholar, vitalized by a particular vision and a will to succeed, will use the reviewing opportunity to stake out his or her own claim at the expense of the author under review. Editors need good sense and some luck to find the right "first reviewers," and they should avoid the temptation to send books to their own and their colleagues' students solely as a way of enhancing their vitas.

II

Looking back at Historical Drama, *I now
ask myself why I received an uncommonly
large number of reviews (some thirty or more)
in a variety of scholarly journals, yet not a
single one in a public journal such as the*
New York Times, TLS, *or the* New Republic. *How is it that several editors apolo-
gized for receiving a string of refusals from a
succession of prospective reviewers? What
motivates an editor to allocate scarce space to a
review, and what motivates a reviewer to allocate scarce time to writing one? Are these
considerations purely intellectual (suitability
of the book to the journal's readership, suitability of the reviewer to the subject, the desire of editor or reviewer to stir up serious
debate), or do personal considerations play a
role (the editor's or the reviewer's need to recompense the author—or the latter's friends—
for past favors or slights, or the reviewer's
perception of possible future rewards from the
author—or the latter's friends—for coming
through with a positive All-Outer)?*

HERBERT LINDENBERGER

Wherein do editors differ in their crite-
ria for reviews from authors, publishers, reviewers, and readers?
First, in the sense of the particular journal they edit, which means
their sense both of the focus of the periodical and of the interests
of its readers. *Boundary 2* and *Signs* want different kinds of
assessments, proceeding from different kinds of assumptions
and focusing on different aspects of the argument about, say, a
new book on realism and the English novel, than do *Victorian
Studies* and *Etudes Anglaises*. That sense of the differing character
of the journal and its audience will lead to differing decisions

about which books to review, how much space to allot to each, how prominent the review will be, and who will do the reviewing, though it must be repeated that all the decisions will in turn be modified by such factors as I've already mentioned—access to a review copy, timely return of the typescript, and so on.

Second, paramount for editors is the reliability of the reviewer. Reliability in this sense extends beyond such primary considerations as the candidate's reputation and knowledge of the field, genre, or author to such undecidables, partly resolved by past experience, as will the assignment be accepted, will it be completed, will it be submitted on time, will it need a lot of editorial tinkering, will it be balanced and fair and sympathetic and unpartisan? (Or, in some cases, will it be brilliantly and provocatively unbalanced and unfair and unsympathetic and partisan, but almost certainly vex the author and readers into thought?) As any editor of a periodical, or for that matter any editor of a publishing house looking for readers to evaluate manuscripts, will attest, the issue is not simply who is the best reader of this essay or monograph, but also (and in pragmatic terms the more important issue) who will get the job done?

Third, editors must pay attention to balance. Authors and publishers may not care whether a particular issue or volume covers a representative range of books and topics, so long as their works are reviewed. And probably most readers read selectively among reviews, never noticing whether the review section as a whole has any coherence or pattern to it. But editors care. And the more general and powerful the journal is, the more editors *must* care, simply to survive. The editors of the *New York Times Book Review* and the *TLS* cannot afford either to include, or to exclude, every feminist critique, or to review only commercial, or only university press, publications. Editors worry too about the mix of reviewers: ideally, any issue should contain some evaluations by senior faculty, some by junior, some by scholars, some by critics, some by theoreticians (with due regard to the competing theories currently vying for attention), some by generalists, some by specialists, and even some from each of the regions of the country, insofar as regional differences are discernible in critical stances.

And finally, editors have some responsibility to be imaginative in their assignments. Not every book on Pound can be reviewed by Hugh Kenner; why not try a Whitman expert, or an art historian interested in early modernism? And not every biography can be reviewed by Richard Ellmann or Leon Edel. Maybe the editor of the letters of one of the biographee's contemporaries would provide an interesting slant, or maybe a famous diarist would, or maybe the most illuminating assessment will come from a historian or a writer or even someone who has succeeded in the same line of endeavor—George Bush reviewing a life of Hubert Humphrey, for instance, or Tom Stoppard on the plays of Neil Simon, or Adrienne Rich on a new biography of Emily Dickinson. It may be true that the more specialized the topic, the less opportunity for such fertilizing cross-references; but even in the most constricted fields a resourceful and persuasive editor will find stimulating matchups. These may not be what the author or the publisher would predict, nor even what the public would expect. But part of the editor's job is not only to find the right reviewer but also to enable that reviewer to write something vital.

Finally, it must be admitted that with few exceptions the review editor lodges far down on the editorial, and even on the general academic, totem pole. Reviews seem to be a necessary part of the system, an unavoidable static amidst the broadcast of ideas. Publishers nevertheless decry the cost of review copies and the paucity of good copy that results; authors—as Wayne Booth testifies[6]—magnify the slights and the put-downs and the misrepresentations and seldom acknowledge the competence and generosity of their critics; and readers, if they have as much spite in them as La Rochefoucauld's maxim predicts, prefer a hatchet job to yet another bland and balanced assessment. Or if not a hatchet job, then a review that tells enough about the book so one doesn't have to go out and buy it.

Reviews are a necessary consequence of the democratization of learning, the transfer of patronage from the aristoi to the demos. With the institutionalization of learning since the late nineteenth century, they have also become a part of the process of certifying the professoriat, and more broadly, of conferring distinction on the intelligentsia. Because of the built-in feedback in the system—reviewer today, reviewee tomorrow—reviewing is rarely an uninhibited exercise of intellectual evaluation. And yet editors share with authors, publishers, and readers the desire for good reviews, ones that are informed about the subject, accurate in their description of the work's achievement, perceptive about the contribution made, tough-minded about its faults, and fair. When all this is combined with a flair for writing, the result is an essay anyone may value. And such reviews, though infrequent, justify the whole enterprise.

Notes

1. Wayne C. Booth, "Three Functions of Reviewing at the Present Time," in *The Horizon of Literature*, ed. Paul Hernadi (Lincoln: Univ. of Nebraska Press, 1982), pp. 261–81, esp. pp. 263–67. The words are Booth's, but not the accidentals, as he capitalizes and italicizes them as headings and elaborates them further in the paragraphs that follow.
2. Lindenberger, "Re-viewing the Reviews of *Historical Drama*," in *The Horizon of Literature*, pp. 283–98, esp. pp. 283–85. I summarize Lindenberger's criteria here, and quote my summaries hereafter.
3. Bloom, "Inescapable Poe," *New York Review of Books*, 11 October 1984, p. 23.
4. Lindenberger, p. 296.
5. See especially James O. Hoge and James L. W. West III, "Academic Book Reviewing: Some Problems and Suggestions," *Scholarly Publishing* 11 (1979):35–41; many of my observations repeat points made by the founding editors of *Review*.
6. Booth, p. 262.

The epigraphs come, respectively, from "The War between Writers and Reviewers," *New York Times Book Review*, 6 January 1985, p. 3; "Reviewmanship," *The Nation*, 22 December 1984, pp. 683–84; and "Reviewing the Reviews of *Historial Drama*," in *The Horizon of Literature*, p. 295.

Bruce D. Macphail

Book Reviews and
the Scholarly Publisher

John Keats, the promising young romantic poet, was hastened to an early grave by savage book reviews. So contended his friend and eulogist, Percy Bysshe Shelley. Though not always so unsympathetically regarded, book reviews are generally not appreciated as fully as they deserve to be.

A thoughtful, timely, well-written book review serves the shared interests of scholarly publishers and the scholarly community. For publishers, the benefits of book reviews are at least twofold: book reviews function as a method of promotion by bringing new books to the attention of readers likely to be interested in them, and they also provide publishers with an evaluation of the fruits of their efforts. Readers look to book reviews for news and appraisal of the latest work being done in their fields of specialty. Very often reviews suggest directions in which further study might proceed; this, in turn, stimulates research and future publication and the continued growth and advance of scholarship. If publishers may be said to be on the frontiers of knowledge, then book reviewers surely help to scout those new frontiers.

In order to fulfill their role in the advancement and dissemination of knowledge and, ultimately, to survive financially, scholarly presses must truly be publishers: they must *publish*, or make known, the books they produce and distribute. Two of the most popular methods of making known or promoting new books, space advertising and direct mail promotion, face significant problems and limitations, especially for the scholarly publisher. Most university presses and nonprofit scholarly publishers, with small advertising and promotional budgets, cannot afford to repeat their space advertisements often enough to be genuinely effective, and surely not on a scale to compete with large, commercial publishers. Moreover, readers are daily bombarded with space advertising, much of it expensive and professionally produced, for all sorts of other products. Most scholarly publishers can expect their space advertising to serve as notice of their continuing interest and activity in particular fields of study, but not to promote the sales of specific books effectively and economically.

Similar problems exist in the use of direct mail promotional literature. With the wide availability of academic, library, and other mailing lists, commercial textbook and trade publishers, as well as scholarly presses, send out reams of promotional literature annually. Much of it is broadly aimed at teachers in broad discipline areas (English, American history, sociology, etc.), or at acquisitions librarians at many different levels and in many kinds of libraries. The result is that professors too often find their mailboxes filled with material, much of it at best of peripheral interest. Acquisitions librarians polled by publishers and publishing consultants in recent years repeatedly say that most of the direct mail literature they receive inevitably, of necessity, winds up in the wastebasket. Such must be the fate of countless carefully designed, expensive fliers. Most publishers are satisfied with a response of 1 to 2 percent on a promotional mailing; anything higher is considered very good.

The publisher's descriptive information in space advertisements and direct mail literature is moreover often regarded, rightly or wrongly, as suspect. At its worst, promotional copy may be a transparent sales pitch. But even when the copy simply describes the contents of the book, without endless strings of honorifics, there is usually an effort to suggest, however subtly, that publisher and author believe the work to be truly important and necessary. In either case, the audience, considering the source of the endorsement, is understandably wary. If quotations from prepublication reviews or other testimonials are employed in the promotional copy, these words, too, are often suspect, since they may have been carefully edited to single out the most glowing praise.

This is not to suggest that space advertising and direct mail promotion are entirely without value. They are important and effective means of promoting the general visibility of a press and its books, and few publishers would attempt to eliminate either from their marketing efforts. Book reviews, however, can serve some of the same promotional ends and provide additional benefits to publishers, authors, readers, and the scholarship they seek to serve.

The actual costs of a publisher's efforts to get his books reviewed are certainly no more than the costs of space advertising or direct mail planned for the same promotional purposes. On an edition of 2,000 copies, for example, a publisher may send out 100 complimentary copies for review. The cost to the publisher is the cost of the books plus postage (staff time and overhead, for purposes of comparison, notwithstanding). Assuming for the purposes of this example a book with a retail price of $20, the unit cost of each book will probably be about $4, perhaps slightly more. Allowing $1 per copy for shipping, the total cost of distributing 100 review copies would be about $500. If the media selected to receive review copies have been carefully chosen, the publisher should be able to expect at least five to ten reviews or notices, often more. The same $500 spent on space advertising in today's inflated market would buy very little, either in size of advertisement or number of insertions, particularly after typesetting and other preparation charges are incurred. Similarly, $500 spent on direct mail promotion would allow for only a modest flier and limited distribution after production, list rental, postage, and fulfillment costs.

Moreover, a book review can be a much more effective promotional device than an advertisement or direct mail piece. Most scholars carefully read the review sections of journals in their fields of interest. They have a very real stake in knowing what is being written, to benefit their teaching and research and to compete in the publish-or-perish environment. Librarians, though not in full agreement on their preferences among review

media, usually cite book reviews above advertisements, catalogues, and promotional literature as the means by which they
select books for purchase for their library's collection. In one
survey of public and university libraries, published in the *Huenefeld Report*, responding librarians most frequently cited "book
reviews" and "general appeal of subject matter" as the two
factors that most influenced their purchasing decisions. When
asked to rank the most useful sources of information about
forthcoming books, librarians chose the Forecasts section of
Publishers Weekly and reviews in *Library Journal* by a margin of
more than four to one over direct mail from publishers. As the
basis for a decision to purchase, "the publisher's description of
the book" failed to get a single vote from the librarians surveyed.[1]

Book reviews are generally regarded as more credible than the
publisher's advertising and promotional copy. A book review in
a scholarly journal usually represents the opinion of someone
recognized as an authority or informed professional in the field.
The review may not always be without bias, but the reader is
usually able to recognize it and, if necessary, compensate for it.
And the complete review is present, not just a flattering excerpt
selected by the publisher.

Purposes other than purely promotional are also served by
book reviews. They often help to shape editorial decisions and
guide the direction of future publishing. When considering a
manuscript for publication, most university presses employ a
screening process that may include an in-house reading, review
by a standing editorial board or faculty committee, and reports
by outside readers chosen for their expertise in the subject of the
manuscript under consideration. This screening largely determines which manuscripts will ultimately be undertaken for publication, and thus provides a form of quality control concerned
with both the scholarly qualities of a given proposal and its
appropriateness in the publisher's list.

The reviews that appear after a book has been published differ
most obviously from prepublication readers' reports in that the
latter deal with the original manuscript—the unedited, unim-

proved effort—and not the final product. The review is, in effect, often of a substantially different work, presumed to be the best effort of author and publisher working together. As such, it is an evaluation not merely of the scholarly merit of the work (already believed to be sufficient to warrant publication) but also to the degree to which author and publisher have succeeded in eliminating the deficiencies and shortcomings noticed before publication. It is a review of the publishing process as well as of the published work.

Many publishers tend to return repeatedly to a familiar and often rather small pool of prepublication readers to assist with manuscript evaluation. In some respects, this practice is quite justifiable: the publisher knows the strengths and biases of these readers from past experience, and can select from among them and weigh their opinions accordingly. The readers, in turn, become increasingly familiar with the publisher's editorial needs and desires, and can offer judgments that take into consideration the strengths and weaknesses of the house's list and also its publishing philosophy. But repeated use of the same readers, and increased familiarity between publisher and reader, can also unfairly circumscribe or bias judgments. The pool of postpublication reviewers will likely be larger than that from which the publisher customarily selects his outside readers. The sheer number of reviewers evaluating a published work ensures a much wider range of opinion, and some books that had no difficulty securing approval for publication may be found to be flawed or—and this is always more pleasant—a book that squeaked through the editorial committee may earn high praise.

It is a sad commentary that, in many publishing houses, problems and shortcomings cited in reviews seem to be taken more seriously than similar criticisms made in private correspondence or in-house commentary. Inaccuracies, omissions, oversights, even typographical errors that have slipped through the editorial process suddenly lose their anonymity when pointedly noticed in print. Publishers deal in the published word, and hence tend to respect it more than any other form of criticism.

A good book review can be more than just a round of academic applause, with gentle (or not so gentle) chidings of error and deficiency. Perceptive reviewers often go beyond analysis of the work to compare it with other works in the field, and, more important, to suggest directions in which further study should proceed. Alert and aggressive editors and authors, in turn, act on these suggestions, and the growth of knowledge is given a new impetus. Since book reviews can serve the scholarly world, publishers and readers alike, in so many useful ways, it behooves the scholarly publisher to give serious attention to the process of getting his books reviewed. How, then, do publishers go about securing reviews?

The cardinal rule most publishers follow is: "Learn the review media." There are a number of ways in which this can be approached. Perhaps the most obvious sources of information are reference books and directories. *Literary Market Place* has sections listing the names and addresses of the major magazines, journals, and newspapers published in the United States, citing in most cases the name of the book review editor and often some guidelines as to the sorts of books reviewed. In a separate listing, the magazines and journals are classified by subject interest. *Ulrich's International Periodicals Directory* provides a more comprehensive list of media, with circulations ranging from the hundreds to the millions, from all parts of the world. *Ulrich's* is arranged by subjects (anthropology, architecture, art, business and economics, chemistry, education, etc.), making it relatively easy to scan the media in a particular field for appropriate prospects. The citations indicate whether the medium carries book reviews, whether advertising is accepted, and the language of publication, together with other information. An alphabetical index allows the user to locate the primary entry as well as cross-references for any given publication. *Ayer's Directory of Periodicals* and the *Editor and Publisher International Yearbook* are organized geographically. *Ayer's* includes only U.S. and Canadian publications; the *Editor and Publisher International Yearbook* lists publications outside North America. The last two publications are most useful in selecting possible review media for books of regional interest, or for identifying publications in a particular location such as the author's home town. All these reference books are issued in new editions annually.

Most scholarly presses tend to concentrate their publishing in a few fields of study. The staff member responsible for deciding where to send review copies, usually the publicity or promotion manager, will generally obtain sample copies of journals to which the press does not already subscribe. The actual journal tells far more than any directory listing can about its policies and interests, and its potential for publishing reviews.

Publishing colleagues also provide assistance. Many editors routinely read the academic journals in the fields in which they are seeking to acquire manuscripts, and can advise on the differences among journals publishing in similar or related fields. Advertising managers can provide readership profiles and statements of editorial policies and interests, received from media trying to sell space. But it is the author above all who is likely to know the most important journals in his field, and who may also know individual reviewers who can place reviews in specific journals. Authors sometimes are puzzled or annoyed at being asked to list possible review media; but the request is made because of their years of specialized experience, and they should recognize that it is made in their interests and not from any laziness on the publisher's part.

A thorough publicity manager determines the name and address of the book review editor for each medium to which review copies are regularly sent, and the names and addresses of freelance writers and reviewers who regularly contribute to appropriate media. These important contacts are kept informed of what the press is doing through regular mailings of catalogues and other announcements. Some editors and reviewers will write to the publisher and request specific books they have noted in these mailings. Publications with large circulations and great influence are less likely to ask for specific review copies; they receive, unsolicited, more than they can use. To secure reviews in such major media, the publisher must ascertain their special interests, send them appropriate books for review, and—mostly—try through personal attention to keep them interested in the press and its list. The publicity manager must also be aware of any special policies: certain media, such as the Forecasts section of *Publishers Weekly*, will review only from advance page proofs or prepublication copies of forthcoming books; others, such as *Choice*, will review only from finished books.

Most publishers making a serious effort to get their books reviewed find themselves dealing with a large number of review media in many different fields of interest. If these are to be approached systematically, and the results tracked for future reference, a file and recordkeeping system is essential. Every publisher may approach this differently, but some elements at least will be common to all. The system we employ at the University of Oklahoma Press is one such approach.

Each review medium—journal, newspaper, radio station, etc.—is given a separate sheet, on which are listed the name and address of the book review editor or of any other person to whom review copies should be sent. The address may differ from that of the editorial office: some people prefer to receive review copies at home; some book review editors of academic journals teach on campuses distant from their journal's editorial office. Each file entry also notes the subjects of interest to the reviewer or medium, and may contain additional information such as circulation, frequency of publication, and average number of books reviewed per issue or per year.

On each sheet the person responsible for distributing review copies (or a clerical assistant) records the books sent to that medium for review, and the dates they were sent. The sheets are filed by categories—magazines and journals, free-lance reviewers (and "others"), newspapers, and broadcast media. The first two categories are filed alphabetically by name; newspapers and broadcast media are filed by state to facilitate regional distribution of review copies.

The complete file of names and addresses constitutes a comprehensive directory of those media of primary importance to the press. The file is more complete and more current than any directory, or even several directories. It affords quick, uniform, centralized access to regularly used information, eliminating the need to search repeatedly through several directories and other sources and thereby minimizing the possibility of clerical error in preparing mailing labels. It also serves as a record of review copies sent, and can be used as a mailing list for catalogues and other promotional material. For all but the largest publishers, the file can be kept on index cards or letter-sized sheets, as described above. Those publishers who have access to a versatile computer system may be able to use the computer to help maintain the file, generate mailing labels, and keep records of review copies sent.

Like any other system or directory, the review media file must, of course, be kept up to date. The names and addresses of book review editors and media change; some media cease publication; new media appear; existing media begin to carry book reviews or modify their reviewing policies. Very often the book review editor reports such changes, which are then entered in the file. The Media section of *Publishers Weekly* carries news of such changes as well. We also scan each new edition of the major reference works previously mentioned for any changes that may have gone unreported or unnoticed.

As the number of entries increases, it becomes increasingly awkward and time-consuming to comb through the entire file searching for media in a particular subject area. We therefore have prepared a subject index for each of the areas in which the press publishes. This is simply a list of review media in a particular field, with a brief note added to each entry to distinguish its special interest or focus. We also have indexes for "general interest" media (major national magazines and journals, such as the *New York Review of Books* or the *American Scholar*), book review syndicates (such as Kirkus or John Barkham Reviews), and newspapers, which do not readily lend themselves to classification by subject.

If the review media have been selected with care, and review copies have been sent regularly, systematically, and appropriately, reviews should begin to appear. Most publishers routinely ask for two copies of any review, but these are not always forthcoming. Other channels may have to be employed. The press's own staff will spot reviews while reading in their fields of interest. Some presses employ a professional clipping service, such as Luce or Burrelle, which scans the media and sends the publisher copies of any reviews or notices. When a review appears, it is noted in the review media file, simply by entering its date of publication next to the record that the review copy was sent. Over time, it becomes easy to determine which media are reviewing the books they are sent, and how quickly. If review copies are regularly sent to a particular medium and are never reviewed, we will get in touch with the book review editor and try to determine if there is a problem. We may discover that the review copies were being sent to the wrong address, that the medium no longer carries book reviews, or that there is some other misunderstanding. The very inquiry sometimes attracts increased attention to our books.

The record of success or failure that emerges from the review media file system is of great benefit to someone who is new to the job of sending out review copies, or to anyone who must learn about the media in a hitherto unfamiliar field. Even a seasoned professional can learn a great deal by keeping such records instead of relying solely upon memory or subjective impressions.

Most presses keep the review clippings for future reference. One copy is normally sent to the author, not only as a matter of courtesy but also to let him know what his publisher is doing to promote interest in his book. Reviews also are circulated to the director, editors, marketing personnel, and other interested staff members at the press.

Authors, editors, and reviewers can all contribute to the effectiveness and value of book reviews. Authors and editors can help by suggesting appropriate review media to the person responsible for review copy distribution. Reviewers and book review editors should endeavor to make their interests known to publishers, request review copies of significant new books, encourage prompt publication of serious book reviews,[2] and send copies of those reviews to the publisher. Communication and cooperation serve all concerned—author, publisher, reviewer, and reader. Book reviews help to disseminate information, and to evaluate and encourage scholarship; these are goals toward which we all strive.

Notes

This essay originally appeared in the October 1980 issue of *Scholarly Publishing* and is reprinted by permission of the University of Toronto Press.

1. For a complete discussion of this poll of librarians' preferences, see "How Acquisition Librarians Say You Should Deal with Them," in the *Huenefeld Report* (Bedford, Massachusetts: Vinebrook Publications), 2 June 1975.

2. See James O. Hoge and James L. W. West III, "Academic Book Reviewing: Some Problems and Suggestions," in *Scholarly Publishing* 11 (1979):35–41, for further discussion.

Michael West

Reflections on Star Wars and Scholarly Reviewing

Once upon a time, in a galaxy far, far away, I was an untenured assistant professor with little to do in my spare time but feel sorry for myself. In the office of a colleague who edited a journal stood several cardboard cartons where books sent in for review but never assigned (the majority) were unceremoniously dumped for departmental scavenging. A title on top caught my eye, for it was by my dissertation supervisor. Rummaging further for freebies, I found two more on the same subject. The thought popped into my head that perhaps I could expand not only my library but my vita. My colleague benignly granted my request to review the trio. His assistant editor even gave me some wise advice about toning down the adulation all too evident in my treatment of my erstwhile mentor's opus. Sad to say, I largely ignored it. Thus began my not atypical career as a reviewer.

It is not an extensive career. Sprinkled among the three dozen articles and essays itemized in my current vita are a mere nine reviews: a brace each for *The Scriblerian* and *Seventeenth-Century News* (before I decided that the kudos garnered through short notices in such periodicals simply did not recompense me adequately for the effort involved), two more substantial reviews of recent vintage for *Modern Philology* and *Renaissance Quarterly*, and for *College English* a trio of review essays. Were reviewing more honored, I might review more. Whether reviewing should be more honored is, however, a question about which I confess some ambivalence. At a recent convention the head of English at a major Texas university confided in me his perplexity when in their first annual conference a junior member announced his desire to base his scholarly career solely upon academic reviewing. What was he to say? I could understand the raised eyebrows with which he described this request. I could also understand the soul-searching that led him ultimately to decide that if reviewing is a worthwhile form of scholarly endeavor, then it ought in theory at least to be possible to earn tenure simply by doing it very well. Yet while I sympathized with his dilemma and its resolution, a trace of smugness tinged my sympathy. "Reviews may do for tenure down in Texas," I found myself thinking, "but thank goodness tenure committees at Pitt demand more substantial achievements of junior faculty! They'll storm the Alamo with snowballs before I vote to promote on a record consisting solely of reviews."

To check my impressions about the role of reviews in the personnel process, I polled forty deans throughout academe. Sixteen responded to my questionnaire, and the results are summarized in an appendix. For whatever it is worth, all were highly dubious that on their campuses a candidate could earn tenure by reviewing alone. Yet though a faintly patronizing attitude toward reviews tinges many responses, by a two-to-one margin deans agreed that a good academic vita should still itemize reviews individually rather than simply list the journals involved in a summary sentence thus: "Reviews in *College English, The Scriblerian, Seventeenth-Century News*." I was pleased and surprised to have my own instincts thus confirmed, for something has always made me uncomfortable with that common academic practice. "Many reviews are not worthy of publication," observed one acerb dean—so failing to list reviews individually may simply nominate them for membership in that group. As far as I am concerned, reviews not worth enumerating bibliographically in a vita are not worth writing.

Only three deans felt that in their personnel process "good scholarly book reviews by a promotion candidate would count almost as much for him as good scholarly notes of the same length." But this distinctly minority opinion may have merit. Certainly my own reviews should not be automatically subordinated en bloc to the value of my "original" scholarly contributions. For example, my periodical bibliography includes two boring little notes: "John Evelyn, Sir Kenelm Digby, and Thoreau's Vital Spirits" and "Shakespeare Allusion in Emily Dickinson." Each corrects a mistake in the learned commentary on a major author by properly identifying the source of a disputed allusion. But several of my reviews do as much or more. Thus reviewing *The Poems of John Dryden, 1693–96,* for *Seventeenth-Century News* gave me the occasion to set the commentary straight on a couple of points. And reviewing that volume of the California *Dryden* not only required far more knowledge on my part but took more time than composing my brief little notes. To assess the relative merits of these various opuscula is perhaps to disregard Dr. Johnson's sage warning not to dispute a point of precedence between a gnat and a flea. But anyone obscenely curious enough to consult them all will, I think, form a more accurate and favorable impression of my intellectual abilities from the review than from either of these notes.

It simply won't do to assume that any published note represents a "contribution to knowledge" of a higher order than any review. The two scholarly genres often overlap, and the better reviews sometimes contain original scholarly contributions that would be separately publishable as notes. (T. S. Eliot's epochal essay "The Metaphysical Poets" was, after all, simply a review of a scholarly anthology for *TLS.*) Specialized bibliographies may reflect this fact by citing particularly authoritative reviews of a scholarly book together with the reference to the book itself. For this reason my vita does not list my reviews separately from notes and articles. Doing so would falsify the continuity of aim and procedure that I would like to think unites them all as "scholarship."

Moreover, such a segregated vita would misrepresent the nature of my scholarly reputation, for that may now rest upon a review more than upon any article I have written. In 1980, after some prompting on my part, *College English* asked me to review the *MLA Directory of Periodicals* and *Scholarly Communication: The Report of the National Enquiry.* With one eye on Macaulay's efforts for the *Edinburgh Review* (and those who ably continue that tradition for *TLS* and the *New York Review of Books* today), I produced a review essay in which the assigned books became the springboard for my own analysis of the topic at hand. My essay concluded with a tabular ranking (i.e., a review) of about two hundred journals in English studies, which attracted considerable attention. When the *Directory of American Scholars* recently solicited a fresh entry from me, I felt no hesitation in selecting this review essay as one of the most influential pieces I've written. My guess is that I'm better known (or more notorious) as its author than as the author of two *PMLA* articles and thirty other specimens of "original scholarship."

In a way, then, it may be possible for a scholar to make a modest reputation mainly as a reviewer. But I would be hard-pressed to name other scholars who have done it. Mine seems a peculiar and unenviable achievement, suspect even to myself. Though more adept scholarly reviewers than I certainly exist, as *TLS* and the *New York Review of Books* regularly remind me, they are generally more eminent scholars as well, so they are primarily known for their original scholarship rather than for their reviewing. John Sparrow comes to my mind as a literary scholar perhaps most widely known for his trenchancy as a reviewer, but I cannot offhand think of another such figure. Since reviews are inevitably parasitic upon more creative literary genres, the paramount respect accorded achievement in those genres is quite understandable. We can imagine a world of books without reviews, but not the reverse. Not only does a review depend upon an original work for its raison d'être—its relative brevity means that the reader cannot always be given ample evidence for the opinions proffered but must rely on the authority of the reviewer, whether attested by an independent reputation, or lacking that, simply by the reputation of the periodical. In freshman composition courses academics spend much time deprecating the argument from authority, but it is an important part of the rhetoric of reviewing. Few of the English teachers who deprecate it could be tempted to attend a movie by an ad that splashed about superlatives in quotation marks—"marvelous," "scintillating comedy"—without attribution. (What a pang shot through me a decade ago, when I saw my words from an early review quoted in a promotional flier for the University of California Press—but with my humble authorship deleted in order to ascribe the praise to the august collective dignity of *The Scriblerian*! Alas, reviewers as well as reviewed sometimes need to be reminded of just where they rank in the cosmos.) Even the *TLS*, for many years the last bastion of the anonymous review, has finally and belatedly caved in. Though their policy of anonymity was "meant to discourage self-indulgence," all it really did was "half-canonize it."[1] It is the peculiar need for externally demonstrable authority in reviewing—for scholarly authority based outside the confines of the review itself—that makes it difficult for young hopefuls in Texas to build academic careers solely upon reviewing.

What are the limits and responsibilities of that authority? The question has been pressing upon my mind in recent months because of a letter from the author of a book that I recently reviewed. It was *The Wisdom of Words: Language, Theology and Literature in the New England Renaissance*, by Philip Gura, now Professor of English, University of North Carolina. Though at that time we had never met, for several years Professor Gura and I had been cultivating the same intellectual field, hailing each other cheerily across the furrows in footnotes, corresponding occasionally, and both reaping a goodly harvest of articles. I had read his dissertation with great profit, so I was a trifle disappointed when the book that emerged from his revisions did not, as it seemed to me, quite do justice to its promise. In my review I praised his book as "provocative" and "worthwhile" but, on the assumption that its virtues could ultimately speak for themselves, devoted somewhat more attention to its questionable aspects. The task was one for which my research certainly qualified me; whether the result was fair-minded and instructive readers must judge for themselves.

They must also judge for themselves the letter that I received from Gura, which he has generously allowed me to reprint in the hope of clarifying larger issues about the nature of reviewing:

Dear Professor West:

I read with considerable interest your recent review of The Wisdom of Words *and want to thank you for taking the time to dissect it so carefully. I appreciate how difficult it must be to address an argument at points quite different from one's own sense of things and yet maintain the standards of civilized discourse, which, for the most part, you manage to do. We simply have a disagreement about the nature of the American Romantics' interest in language. Your strictures notwithstanding, I still believe that the theological dimensions of this interest gave American language study its basic shape. Put bluntly, men like Bushnell and Emerson got their notions of symbolic language from Coleridge and not from Stewart.*

I also should say that I learned much from your review, and for that as well I thank you. Your understanding of eighteenth-century language study admittedly is more profound than mine. I would point, out, however, that, since you seem to find Professor Aarsleff's "oral" comment to me so telling, he was one of the scholars who read the manuscript (approvingly) for Wesleyan, as did others whose expertise in the field is not in question. I am not embarrassed by what you consider my oversights. I set out to bring an important topic to the attention of literary historians and succeeded in that task. All reviews, including yours, testify to that fact.

One last point. I found the overall sharpness of your review quite surprising, particularly given the generosity with which I always have treated your pioneering essays.

Sincerely yours,
Philip Gura

These sentiments probably stir an echo in the bosoms of many scholarly authors with no interest in the American Renaissance. At least four of the points succinctly raised by Gura merit careful and more generalized reflection by anyone interested in the art of reviewing.

While we certainly have a disagreement about "the American Romantics' interest in language," I'm not sure that "we simply have a disagreement." Having been more warmly reviewed in a dozen other journals, Gura seems understandably prone to see ours as a difference of "opinion." But it's not, really, for his "opinions" rest upon two hundred pages of careful argumentation—though not quite careful enough, as I tried to demonstrate in my review but perhaps only wound up suggesting. Likewise my "opinions" rest upon a massive investigation of the evidence, some of which I have published elsewhere, some of which is still forthcoming. What permits this to seem a difference of opinion is the fact that *Modern Philology* put only three pages at my disposal. I hope that I did more than most reviewers to supply the evidence on which my judgments were based, but even exceeding the imposed limits did not allow for much evidence. Mine was the classic dilemma of the scholarly reviewer: how to achieve intellectual credibility without space.

To improve the quality of reviewing, editors will have to encourage somewhat longer reviews. Many journals could find space for them simply by eliminating the weakest article (or the weakest review) from each issue. Killing two birds with one stone, this would improve not only reviewing but scholarship, for it should be obvious to any thoughtful observer that literary studies are glutted with soi-disant scholarship but suffer from a poverty of critical self-evaluation. Indeed, the other reviews of Gura's book exemplify this tendency. One of the shakier sections of the book involves the claim that in Thoreau's description of a sandbank in *Walden*, "All ends in those dental sounds—'the symbols of death' as Kraitsir called them: l-e-a-f, g-l-o-b-e, l-i-f-e" (p. 135). As I pointed out in my review, Gura's examples here involve no sounds that we would classify as dentals, so his mistaken phonology renders his startling analysis of Thoreau's prose highly suspect. Anyone competent to review a study of nineteenth-century linguistics should have been capable of picking up this key error, yet I was apparently the only reviewer to criticize this crippling flaw in a stylistic analysis that several naively singled out for praise. Conceivably, he is right to suggest that since about a dozen briefer notices treated his book more favorably, I am guilty of undue sharpness. But from these circumstances it is also possible to conclude that short reviews do not encourage their authors to dig very deeply into books, so that even in relatively strong journals literary scholarship is reviewed rather too indulgently.

Gura's letter also suggests that at points my review transgressed a scholarly canon of good taste. What are "the standards of civilized discourse" from which I lapsed occasionally? Few readers will suppose that the barbarians at the University of Chicago who run *Modern Philology* require much instruction in intellectual etiquette from the Carolina piedmont. But his complaint should not be casually dismissed, for it represents a way of thinking about academic reviewing that—precisely because it is so common—often reduces it to scholarly backscratching. Did he praise my own work generously because it merited praise or in the hope of reciprocal professional "courtesy"? "The great sin in book reviewing is incest," Professor Stanley Kutler of the University of Wisconsin observes from his perspective as editor of *Reviews in American History*. "I'm appalled at the number of times scholars review their close colleagues, or major professors review their own students. It gives book reviewing a bad name."[2] The situation is no different in literary studies, of course, as my debut as a reviewer may suggest. A friend of mine lunching with some Spenserians at a convention was ruefully amused when over the antipasto two figures arranged to review each other's books in journals to which they controlled entree. What makes the anecdote striking is not that such puffery goes on but that it goes on so shamelessly with no need to conceal it. The conception of scholarly courtesy as reciprocal backscratching is more deeply rooted in the world of letters than elsewhere. Comparing personnel evaluation in the humanities with the sciences, one dean commented, "You have to watch out more for ritual politeness: they write for close readers and may try to help friends a little too much." Florid scholarly compliments date back at least to the Neo-Latin commentaries of Renaissance humanists, and a tradition of effusive academic politeness still flourishes with special vigor in areas like Italian studies.

Scholarly reviewing is the poorer for this tradition, which breeds not only dishonesty but boredom. Though the best journalistic reviews can be brilliantly entertaining, too many scholarly reviewers write like disciples of McLuhan in the apparent conviction that the tedium is the message. As R. S. Wolper points out, the undertow of cliché often sets in with the opening sentence, when the academic reviewer hails a book that is " 'a penetrating close analysis of . . .'; 'has at last done belated justice to . . .'; 'does scholarship a service by . . .'; 'makes us look forward to. . . .' "[3] Unless the tendency to such formulaic phrasing is vigorously resisted from the outset, the result is likely to be another depressing specimen of constipated academic panegyric. In his book Gura argued that minor figures like James Marsh and Horace Bushnell were "quite literally the spiritual midwives of the symbolic consciousness in the New England Renaissance" (p. 31). Finding this claim exaggerated, somewhat contradictorily expressed, and a little fuzzy about the chapter's key distinction between literal and figurative language, I quoted it and wrote that on the evidence presented Marsh "seems not so much an independently practising midwife (whether literal or spiritual) as a student nurse assistant to Drs. Coleridge, Kant, Herder, and Schelling." The criticism amused me, I confess, and I hoped it would amuse others. If two or three witticisms like this represent unseemly levity, then I am afraid that I disgraced my judicial robes.

Likewise I did not deny myself the luxury of a couple of sentences editorializing on favorite topics, like the pressures for premature publication that make it difficult for junior faculty to hold their books back long enough to refine them. "One can sympathize with the motives that keep a young scholar from adopting such a course," I wrote, "but one should not condone career pressures by excusing the results." Gura finds my generalizations about motives for publishing superfluous in a review; but though I am happy to welcome him to the state of tenured complacency, I continue to think that standards of civilized discourse can best be maintained by reviewers alert to the larger professional implications of their task and willing to suggest, for example, that not all worthy junior faculty should be urged to publish books.

Indeed, *ceteris paribus*, a good scholarly reviewer should command a livelier, wittier, and more biting prose than a good scholarly author needs to wield. The shorter literary forms generally demand more in the way of stylistic pyrotechnics. Reviews are in a sense the prose poems of scholarship—potentially and ideally, at least. As one connoisseur of reviewing has observed, "Wit is the soul of brevity."[4] Style is so peculiarly important in reviewing because of the need to establish intellectual authority without extensively marshaling evidence. To gain a reader's confidence within the constricted space at his disposal, a reviewer can use a flair for language to dramatize the standards of taste, learning, judgment, and creativity that he brings to the book under review. If a movie is advertised as "a laff riot," that anonymous blurb disqualifies itself stylistically, at least so far as I am concerned. Likewise an anonymous blurb might conceivably carry conviction if it demonstrated a real gift for phrase-making. For this reason, at the upper levels of journalism good reviews are often more interesting than the ephemera to which they are consecrated. I cannot be the only reader of *New York Magazine* who subscribes out of special relish for the contributions of such reviewers as John Simon, David Denby, John Leonard, and Rhoda Koenig. Their pages are almost invariably entertaining, stimulating, and instructive even when I have only minimal interest in the works under review.

It's curious that so few scholarly journals follow the example of many magazines in recognizing the talents of their reviewers by honoring them with staff appointments. But review editors might be able to recruit more distinguished scholars with a knack for reviewing if a select few were given a title and guaranteed space in every issue to review books of their choice—a column, so to speak. The sort of mild status that now goes with being selected to do a long annual review of the literature in a field would then be parceled out over four quarterly issues in a way that might do more to build subscriber loyalty. If the scholars involved were sufficiently eminent and adept, their qualifications to review a broad range of books of interest to readers would not be in doubt. And if two scholars writing for the same journal both wanted to review the same book, within limits this would be highly salubrious. Could the honor of being chosen not just as an expert on particular books but as a spokesman for the discipline induce talented academics to consecrate more effort to reviewing, to the point of actually meeting quarterly deadlines? Maybe not. But academic administrators might smile more lavishly and benignly on a scholar who was listed as a leading journal's reviewer in every issue rather than as the author of four reviews a year scattered over four journals. By an overwhelming margin more than 80 percent of deans responding agreed that "little academic credit accrues to [scholarly book reviewing]" and that "a tenure candidate would be better advised to channel his energies into writing original notes and articles." To improve reviewing, we need to improve the way in which academe rewards reviewers, which means securing more respect for reviews in academic personnel decisions.

That is unlikely to occur so long as scholarly reviewers approach their task with the booster mentality so painfully evident in much journalistic book reviewing. "Most reviewers in journalism . . . are more inclined to praise too lavishly than to criticize too stringently," observes the editor of the *Washington Post Book World*, and the justice of that observation is amply confirmed by the revealing comments of other review editors collected in the anthology *Book Reviewing*.[5] "Encouragement should be a book review department's primary objective," asserts the editor of the *Philadelphia Inquirer*'s book section (p. 81). "I do not consider myself a book critic," proudly proclaims a Florida reviewer. "If a book fails to interest me, or is poorly written, I don't review it" (p. 100). Others echo her viewpoint: "Unless it is in the public interest to expose errors or to qualify the reputation of an established writer, it is better to ignore bad books" (p. 135). Thus Doris Grumbach, formerly a senior editor of the *Saturday Review* and literary editor of the *New Republic*, who reviews regularly for the *New York Times Book Review*, believes that it "is a shame to waste space on a negative review" (p. 19), and the power of positive thinking receives a similar endorsement from L. E. Sissman on the basis of his experience reviewing for *The Atlantic* and the *New Yorker*. Nor is this viewpoint confined to journalism, as the editor of one scholarly journal makes plain in advising would-be academic reviewers: "To me, a good review is mainly informative. I look with a jaundiced eye on reviewers as evaluators, and on movie critics, drama critics and the like who think their job is to guard the public's pocketbooks" (p. 175). Little wonder that many academics approach book reviews rather as they do letters of recommendation, fancying themselves morally obliged to say nothing at all if they can't say something nice (though they would be dismayed to find their motives compared to those of commercial hacks and flacks).

It is scarcely surprising that academic administrators have scant respect for reviews when so many are so conceived. In *Historical Journals: A Handbook for Writer and Reviewer*, Dale Steiner endeavors manfully to exalt the dignity of reviewing: "A good review can be read and appreciated for its own sake by someone who has no intention of ever picking up the book in question. Such a review is, in its own way, as informative and valuable as a much lengthier article" (p. 11). But this effort is hamstrung by his underlying conviction that a review is essentially a précis of a single source, so that "writing a book (or film or tape) review is, generally speaking, a more readily accomplished alternative to authoring an article." Though Steiner piously hopes that "the college instructor who is too burdened by classes, the demands of students, and committee assignments to research and write an article (let alone a book) can nonetheless demonstrate continuing intellectual vitality by regularly writing reviews," his candid portrait of the scholarly reviewer as academic also-ran is ludicrously self-defeating. Why deans and chairmen should regard such unenergetic dullards as demonstrating intellectual vitality by performing a largely descriptive task within the competence of their own executive secretaries remains unclear.

Nor is it evident why routinely complimentary summaries by the lower echelons of the profession should help determine who accedes to the higher echelons. A majority of deans agreed that recent decades have witnessed a perceptible administrative tendency to bypass reviews in promotion decisions, especially those to professor, which often take place now upon acceptance or publication of a book endorsed by letters from outside authorities. Eighty-five percent of deans responding said that a detailed letter solicited from an eminent authority would carry more weight in their personnel process than the average scholarly review, and they were unanimous in feeling that solicited letters are more helpful to them than brief reviews in low-level journals. Disappointingly few seemed to agree with one dean who believed that the best personnel reports do not always come from the most distinguished scholars. Perhaps more characteristic was the dean who tartly observed, "Unfortunately, we all know how most reviewers are selected by the Book Review Editor." Perhaps most interestingly, they refused to place more stock in a published review of a book than in a confidential letter from the same reviewer. Although one might argue that the public character of a review renders its judgments more objective and reliable, insofar as they must withstand professional scrutiny, by a two-to-one margin deans rejected this notion. Of course, as some commented, letters may deal with the totality of a candidate's work rather than simply one book. But there also seems to be serious administrative mistrust of reviewers' standards. Though an MLA resolution decries the trend to solicited letters, it is all too understandable, I fear, and one of the main reasons for it is the sluggish laxity of our system for evaluating literary scholarship through reviews.

But, it may be objected, reviews are not written chiefly for the convenience of academic administrators, and should not be. My reservations about Gura's first book apparently did nothing to slow his speedy and well-deserved ascent to a professorship with the recent publication of his second and third. Indeed, his letter raises the intriguing question of precisely what audience a reviewer *is* addressing. In her little pamphlet *Reviewing*, Virginia Woolf mulls over that question. Harold Nicolson is her authority for seeing the reviewer "as something quite different from the critic," and she describes with some approval his claim that as a reviewer he sought to address the authors whom he reviewed rather than degrade himself intellectually by addressing the public.[6] This leads her into a pleasant fantasy about combining the role of critic and reviewer by setting up as a doctor for sick books and offering private consultations to authors. Her husband, Leonard, however, explicitly disagreed with her analysis of the rhetoric of reviewing: "The reviewer, unlike the critic, in 999 cases of 1,000 has nothing to say to the author; he is talking to the reader" (p. 29). "But to *which* reader?" we must still ask. One who has read the book in question? A prospective reader of the book? Or a reader of the periodical who is unlikely ever to read the book and indeed relies on the review to relieve him of that task?

Obviously the periodical for which one is reviewing defines one's audience to a considerable extent. Thus a brief notice in *American Anthropologist* found Gura's book "linguistically parochial" (though it did not specifically mention his mistaken phonology) because its reviewer approached it with an anthropological audience's linguistic sophistication in mind. Journals focusing upon American history and literature were noticeably warmer about it, while perhaps most enthusiastic of all were the four journals in religious studies. Clearly the same book can properly have different value for different groups of scholars.

That very fact, however, complicates the task of a reviewer like me, charged with reviewing it for a distinguished omnibus journal covering many kinds of philological inquiry. For whom was I writing? My prose strained to embrace at least seven disparate audiences with conflicting desires:

1. Philip Gura himself, my esteemed intellectual co-worker and potential reviewer someday

2. Deans, chairmen, and academic administrators with the responsibility for promoting Gura in a timely manner, compensating him equitably, or conceivably even hiring him away someday

3. Gura's publisher, which wants its books praised but also wants to know when faulty proofreading jeopardizes its list

4. A small circle of experts who crave every scrap of information on the topic (perhaps no more than a dozen fanatical scholars, some of whom have already read the book and a few of whom may not yet exist), for whom my review will have the archival status of a note since I have already cited it in a subsequent article for *ELH* and future bibliographies may incorporate it with their reference to Gura's volume; these fellow investigators want information more than evaluation, but since they will all read the book anyway what they want most from me is new and essentially pejorative information, a record of Gura's mistakes, omissions, and misemphases that his own pages do not automatically provide

5. Americanists with limited expertise on the topic, who either have read the book already and want help evaluating its theses or—more likely—want me to summarize and evaluate the book so they can decide whether they need to read it; the first group is more interested in defects, the second in virtues

6. A few scholars outside American studies who would normally ignore the book but want to be alerted to works that are either of unusual importance or of unusual pertinence to their own intellectual interests in other areas

7. A number of scholars in other fields who have no intention of ever reading the book but rely on reviews to keep them abreast of what is happening in other sectors of the profession by summarizing and evaluating current scholarship from a broader perspective, probably including most of the scholars who subscribe to journals as individuals, a key group that represents the difference between life and death for many scholarly journals, and keeping them happy requires witty reviewers, among other features

To these seven demanding audiences four more might be added, for my review was also addressed in varying ways to the editors of *Modern Philology*, to my chairman, to myself, and to God. At least in my view, they all presume that so long as I draw the breath of life I should not write like an academic robot. Keeping them all happy is my most difficult task. But even reviewers who limit their attention to the other seven audiences will find it no mean rhetorical and intellectual challenge to meet all the needs of their very diverse readership in a thousand words or less. The author wants to be sympathetically praised for his achievement, of course, but also needs to be counseled honestly for the benefit of his future work. Presses want rave reviews but also want to know when to print errata slips. Administrators want accurate, rigorous evaluation, but often seem to care little about information, and rather distrust humor. Fellow experts can do their own evaluating but want new information about the topic. The average scholar in the discipline may want a neutral presentation of the author's views, but that must somehow be coupled with advice about whether the book is worth reading. Scholars outside the discipline want the reviewer to provide a camera's-eye view of the action within it, yet switch on occasion to a distorting lens that makes for amusing and entertaining reading. And while they especially want to please the last two groups, editors may also want their journal to be known as the home of authoritative analytic reviews, which means that they must meet the standards of the much smaller group of expert investigators reasonably often to satisfy the academic libraries that probably buy the bulk of the subscriptions. The audience for the average scholarly article, by contrast, is much more homogeneous in its intellectual expectations, much less complexly involved in the emotional rhetoric of the piece.

To the extent that my review was addressed to Gura, the fact that he chose to respond to me reflects both its success and its failure. As Virginia Woolf would wish, I have established a private dialogue with the author, but not quite the dialogue I would prefer. The fault cannot simply be ascribed to my interlocutor. In my review I pointed out numerous errors of his and suggested that they compromised some of his theses. Alas, I also committed an error of my own. In a footnote he acknowledged receiving advice from the distinguished authority Hans Aarsleff. I too had been in communication with Professor Aarsleff, and in a letter to me he mentioned that he had "told" Gura thus-and-such when consulted. Misled by the ambiguous wording, I stupidly leapt to the conclusion that Aarsleff had "informed" Gura of certain material in personal conversation. "A modest footnote mentions consulting an authority who orally informed him of antecedents to Kraitsir's work in pre-nineteenth-century linguistic scholarship," I wrote. "Thoreau was indeed demonstrably familiar with the Enlightenment scholars Charles de Brosses and Antoine Court de Gebelin (to say nothing of Plato's Cratylus), who also propounded semantic phonologies but found very different meanings inhering in sounds than did Kraitsir. Had Gura investigated such material at first hand and recognized Thoreau's indebtedness to it, he might not have been tempted to attach such overwhelming and implausible importance to the Hungarian." Now I realize that Gura never spoke to Aarsleff but, like myself, simply corresponded with him. So far as I can see, my error was neither material to my argument nor necessarily derogatory to Gura; I threw in the word "orally" only to clarify that the "authority" he consulted was no published work but a person.[7] An error it was, however, and as Gura's errors impeach his credibility as an author, so ought my error to impeach mine as a reviewer.

Happily, this essay gives me the opportunity to acknowledge my mistake publicly. But only the fortuitous coincidence that I had an essay to write makes that possible, I fear. Suppose Gura had directed his letter to the editors of *Modern Philology*. Would they have been eager to print it? Frankly, I doubt it. Scholarly editors seem reluctant to devote space to such exchanges. I believe that my review was a good one as reviews go—indeed, perhaps the only genuinely authoritative review that Gura's book received. And if even a good review like mine contains a mistake, there must be many more mistakes in the mediocre reviews that abound in the profession. Yet how seldom in scholarly journals does one see an academic complaining about a poor review! It happens, to be sure, but offhand I can think of only a few instances.

In this respect scholarly authors seem to be governed by a tradition of stoic fortitude, and editorial practice encourages their gentlemanly tendency to cultivate a stiff upper lip. One can understand why editors might fear that encouraging such corre-spondence could generate more heat than light. But if authors were more willing and more able to challenge their reviewers publicly, literary scholarship as a whole would benefit. When the *Bulletin of the Midwest Modern Language Association* invited a bevy of distinguished scholars to review the reviews of their own books for a special issue, the results were often highly instruc-tive. Though Wayne C. Booth there avers that authors' laments "almost always sound petty and self-serving," his essay and others demonstrate how much can be learned when authors respond to their reviewers. And he is surely wrong to assert that "nobody wants to read such exercises in public purgation."[8] Even the most lugubrious effusions of authorial egotism can offer high popular drama and entertain one hugely as sequels: The Empire Strikes Back! I can't be the only reader of the *New York Review of Books* who sometimes commences with the letters to the editor. Indeed, the vitality of that forum, I am convinced, plays an essential role in maintaining the extremely high level of reviewing throughout that periodical. True, in disputes with authors reviewers do seem to have the edge, for I find myself scoring most debates in their favor. But there are a goodly number of illuminating draws, and sometimes an author does succeed in overcoming the rhetorical awkwardness of his posi-tion and clearly exposing the reviewer's incompetence or bias. That possibility is salutary for all concerned—authors, readers, *and* reviewers—for being asked to review can tempt one to various kinds of self-indulgence. Just as authors need more vig-orous criticism from reviewers, so scholarly reviewers need more vigorous criticism from authors.

Indeed, I now find myself wondering again about my own motives in reviewing Gura. Since I have speculated about his motives for publishing, mine in reviewing him are certainly fair game. It would be pleasant to report that as a scholar I was animated by nothing but the loftiest love of truth. But only the incurably naive would believe me, so I shall not lay claim to such purity of motive. Indeed, those who possess it do not necessarily make the best reviewers, for truth's devotees are too often zealots, and many books would be better assigned to jesting Pilate. I hope that my review was inspired by *amor veritatis*, but I know perfectly well that *amour propre* was also involved.

Self-interest reinforced the negative tenor of my review in two respects especially. When I enlisted under Milton's banner for the wars of truth, I did not despair of promotion. Indeed, I had hoped to earn mine on the battlefield. Virtually everything that I have written as a scholar has had as one major objective the advancement of my professional career. If I thought reviewing were merely the generous "service to the profession" that it is often described as being, then I would not engage in it. Period. I review to serve not only my peers but myself, through such minuscule increments to my reputation (read *salary*) as I can generate thereby. And I have come to the conclusion that merely laudatory reviews generate less kudos for the reviewer than do those that adopt a critical stance. Rightly so, I think, for it takes noticeably less ability to produce an adequate summary of a book than a reasonably cogent account of its deficiencies. Please understand that this is not the credo of a self-declared hatchet man. I have been happy when a favorable review was quoted in promotional literature, and I have no desire to become known as a cranky reviewer whom no book can ever please. But insofar as reviewers become known, hatchet jobs may play a disproportionate role in establishing their reputations. David Blum rightly observes that the *New York Review of Books* built its audience by panning with panache, for "in the literary world, the best way to catch the reader's eye is with a blast."[9]

When I review any book, therefore, I have a selfish incentive to find justifiable fault with it. This would worry me more were I not convinced that over the long haul no reviewer will prosper except by demonstrating consistent balance, fairness, and accuracy. And since literary academe is scarcely a dog-eat-dog world (except perhaps in the sense of dog-lick-dog), most of my colleagues must either interpret a reviewer's self-interest differently or resist the selfish temptation to be critical with more saintliness that I can muster.

In addition to this general motive to criticize, I had more

particular incentives for finding fault with Gura's book. We are not only intellectual collaborators but intellectual rivals. Though we share a desire to emphasize the importance of linguistic ideas in the American Renaissance, we disagree on many matters of interpretation and detail. Though I began working on this topic before him, he was the first to gather his ideas into a book, while my book on the subject remains aborning. If I am to write it, I must believe that his book leaves much to be desired. This situation occurs frequently in academic reviewing, and in the scanty literature on the subject it seems to be uniformly deplored. Thus Martin Esslin:

> *If the book is on a specialised subject the chances are that someone known to be specialising in the same subject will be chosen to review it. In theory this should be the ideal solution. In practice it often means that a person who is just about to publish a book on the same subject or just* has *published such a book, is put into the position to try to kill what is, in effect, a rival competitive enterprise. Many are those who are not big enough as personalities to transcend such a temptation. . . . This ability to overcome personal considerations and to remain objective in a matter of such close and emotive immediate concern is the mark of true scholarship and generous humanity. It is, alas, most rare; its opposite almost the rule.* [10]

I cheerfully confess that personal envy, intellectual rivalry, and a sense of academic territoriality may have been involved in my review of Gura's book. But this shames me very little if at all, nor can I join Esslin in seeing all reviewers with such motives as the dark legions of Darth Vader maneuvering their Death Star in for the kill. For human nature is so constituted (at least in my rather Rochefoucauldian view) that virtually all admirable human enterprises are generally pursued for motives that are less than wholly admirable in themselves. Self-interest of various kinds certainly helps to account for many negative reviews. But self-interest of other kinds is equally responsible for many laudatory reviews. How many books are warmly praised by reviewers who know little about the subject partly because routine praise dispatches the reviewer's task more handily than confessing ignorance, let alone working to remedy it? With hindsight, I blushingly confess that such complacent laziness played a discernible part in at least one of my favorable reviews, and I regret its authorship more than I regret anything I have written about Gura. How many other laudatory reviews stem from some sort of party spirit? Blame and praise can both be given for unedifying motives, and in any review selfishness is usually involved to some degree. But detecting it does not invalidate the review, any more than detecting unconscious sadistic impulses in a surgeon invalidates his surgery. Many a good banker is a sublimated anal retentive, Freud would argue, and there are perhaps few great actors without a disturbing tincture of narcissism. Presumably the four cardinal virtues have something to do with the quality of my teaching; but pride, avarice, and other deadly sins also power my classroom performances. Theologically I rely on grace. What counts morally—thank God—is whether individuals can master and direct their selfish drives to achieve some worthwhile social end. Whereas Esslin wants the reviewer to transcend his ego, I will be satisfied if he harnesses it wisely. A book may receive four reviews—two favorable and two unfavorable—all of them partly attributable to selfish motives. Yet the four reviews may consist of one empty rave, one mean-spirited pan, and two excellent pieces with sharply opposed verdicts, both of which may be far superior as reviews to a fifth notice written objectively in utter boredom by the most disinterested observer imaginable.

Whether intellectual rivalry flawed my review of Gura's book or inspired me to an unusually fine performance is thus a question that can be answered only by those who read the book together with all its reviews. I shall merely say that I thought about it considerably when I wrote my review, continue to think about it, and urge any reviewer in such circumstances to consult his conscience carefully. Certainly the possibilities for personal bias are real enough to give one pause. But were I a review editor, I would worry more about assigning a book to, say, any of the authorities cited in the preface as having already read the manu-

script approvingly than I would about assigning it to rival scholars working in the field.

Whether or not intellectual rivalry made mine a good review, I
am convinced that at least some reviews profit from it. Moreover, I think that scholarly reviewing like scholarship as a whole
can benefit from a spirit of intellectual competition, properly
understood. Conceivably my notions of what constitutes a good
review rely too much on adversarial conceptions of truth. But
one cannot appeal from my argument to any generally recognized authority on the subject. It is startling how scanty and
impoverished is the scholarly literature on scholarly reviewing.
Our profession has scarcely begun to reflect on the qualities that
make a good review. Earlier essays in this volume are a welcome
step toward a taxonomy of reviews, for it becomes obvious to
anyone who considers the subject thoughtfully that reviews can
and should be categorized in numerous phyla and subspecies,
each with its own appropriate aims and standards. Likewise my
remarks about the rhetoric of reviewing are really an invitation
to further investigation. But we cannot theorize in a vacuum. If
academe is to improve its reviews, we need some generally
acknowledged models of excellence in the form.

James O. Hoge, the editor of this volume, and James L. W.
West III, one of my fellow contributors to it, also edit *Review*, an
annual dedicated to the improvement of literary reviewing. One
of the best things they could do would be to establish an annual
prize for reviews published anywhere on language and literature.
Working perhaps through the Conference of Editors of Learned
Journals, *Review* could invite editors throughout the literary
disciplines to nominate reviews published in their own journals
as the best received that year. The entire list of distinguished
reviews could appear annually in *Review* and would appropriately recognize scholars for what has hitherto been a largely
thankless and invisible task. Such professional recognition might
begin to earn for reviewers the administrative approval that must
in the long run underpin any effort to improve the quality of
literary reviewing. Then *Review* could appoint a distinguished
panel of judges to scrutinize all entries and select some for modest

awards, perhaps with a brief citation explaining the nature of the winner's excellence in the judges' eyes. Such a process conducted annually for a decade or more would improve standards in this field. Several periodicals sponsor prizes for articles. Why does no periodical to my knowledge sponsor a prize for reviews, though reviews far outnumber articles in many professional journals?

A pipe dream? Perhaps. Certainly the details require thought. But if the editors of *Review* are unenterprising, some editor elsewhere should take matters into his own hands by establishing an award for his own journal. Whoever does should see an improvement not only in the quality of reviews received but, I suspect, in the promptness with which they are submitted. Since some day I hope to publish a book myself, I have an author's vested interest in seeing the appearance of reviews expedited, for now they often appear too late to have any impact on sales. Moreover, if an editor wants my book reviewed speedily, expertly, and intensely, I can think of nobody in this galaxy better qualified for the job than Philip Gura. If and when I publish my book, I am confident that he will treat it with just as much fairness as I tried to accord him. The more rigorous and searching his criticisms, the more he, I, and scholarship stand to benefit. Should there be a prize for reviewing at that point, I sincerely hope that he wins it and lives happily ever after, for my book's sale (like his) will probably benefit from anyone's exercising his wits upon it in a notable way.

Meanwhile, may the Force be with us both!

Appendix

Responses to the following questionnaire were received from administrators at Baruch College-CUNY, Brown University, Duke University, Indiana University, Knox College, Louisiana State University, University of Mississippi, Muskingum College, Notre Dame, University of North Carolina at Greensboro, Oregon State University, Pomona College, University of Rochester, University of South Carolina, University of Texas, and UCLA. Not all administrators answered all questions, and answers to some questions were hedged in a way that makes tabulation a trifle difficult. For whatever it is worth, here is the questionnaire together with such decanal wisdom on the subject of reviewing and personnel evaluation as I have been able to gather.

I. In the past few years the Modern Language Association has gone on record opposing the solicitation of confidential letters from outside authorities as part of the evidence in academic promotion cases. Yet many institutions continue—perhaps for good reason—to rely heavily on such confidential assessments of promotion candidates' work. Does their confidentiality make them more or less reliable than published reviews (of course, in many tenure cases no published reviews are available)? Check any of the following statements that square with your administrative experience, and amplify if necessary.

a) Other things being equal, I would take more stock in a published review of a book than in a confidential letter from the same reviewer.
[Four administrators agreed with this statement; eight disagreed.]

b) A detailed letter solicited from an eminent authority would carry more weight in our personnel process than a review in an average professional journal.
[Eleven administrators agreed and only two disagreed.]

c) In assessing the value of scholarly books, solicited letters generally prove more helpful than brief notices or anonymous reviews in low-level journals.
[Thirteen administrators endorsed this statement unanimously.]

d) A book receiving only poor reviews is probably still a more impressive accomplishment than a book receiving no reviews at all.
[Five deans agreed to some extent with this statement, but eight deans sharply challenged it.]

II. Do the various disciplines differ in the rigor with which their members evaluate each other's work?

a) Admittedly, the role of reviewing in the sciences differs from that in the humanities (for one thing, fewer scientists write books), but in general scientists are more willing to criticize poor work than are humanists.
[Three deans agreed with this statement, three disagreed, three hedged their answers, and many abstained.]

b) In my experience humanistic departments are just as rigorous as departments in the sciences and social sciences in evaluating the quality of work by candidates for promotion.
[Nine administrators agreed with this statement and only

one disagreed. How to reconcile these responses with those to the preceding question is unclear.]

c) Taking into account not merely the departments on my campus but my overall academic experience of the disciplines they represent, some humanistic disciplines seem more rigorous than others in reviewing published work and/or evaluating a candidate's work as part of the promotion process. Among the most rigorous and demanding humanistic disciplines in my experience have been_____.
The least rigorous and demanding humanistic disciplines tend to be_____.
[Several deans took the Fifth Amendment on this one or reminded me of my promise to keep answers confidential. History seems to be reputed the toughest humanistic discipline. Nine deans praised historians for the rigor of their evaluations and only one found them lax. Six deans found philosophers especially demanding while two thought them indulgent. By contrast, the modern foreign languages were cited by eight deans for the unusually low level of standards prevailing, and only a single dean ranked a language among the most demanding disciplines. Reports on English were more mixed: while six deans ranked it with the most demanding humanistic disciplines, it was ranked among the softest by three deans, tying it for second place from the bottom of the totem pole with religious studies.]

d) Though disciplines may differ in the rigor with which they evaluate promotion candidates, they do not seem to differ correspondingly in the rigor with which they review professional books.
[Five administrators thought this statement was true and none denied it, but most declined to hazard an opinion.]

III. What value does the academic personnel process attach to book reviewing?

a) In our personnel process good scholarly book reviews by a promotion candidate would count almost as much for him as good scholarly notes of the same length.
["Not in ours," chorused eight deans, while only three affirmed the statement.]

b) While scholarly book reviewing is a worthwhile professional service, little academic credit accrues to it. A tenure candidate would be better advised to channel his energies into writing original notes and articles, and it is unlikely that an academic could earn tenure on my campus by scholarly book reviewing alone.

[Twelve administrators cheerfully endorsed this statement; three diffidently questioned it to some degree.]

c)   Itemizing one's book reviews individually in a good academic vita is usually superfluous; better simply to append to the bibliography a summary sentence, thus: "Reviews in Journals *X*, *Y*, and *Z*."

[Only two deans agreed with this. Eight opposed it and two more preferred full bibliographic description of selected reviews.]

IV.   Whereas tenure decisions must be made on a relatively fixed schedule, the timing of promotions to full professor is more variable, sometimes coinciding with the completion of a book. Do reviews play the same role in this process that they did a few decades ago? If they are more often discounted now, why?

a)   On my campus we would be more likely to promote to full professor upon acceptance of a book manuscript or immediately upon publication of it rather than waiting for reviews to attest to its quality.

[Eight administrators agreed with this statement, four disagreed, and three professed to be unable to generalize about local practice.]

b)   In past decades academics were more likely to be held in rank until the emergence of reviews, whereas contemporary practice tends to expedite the promotion process by discounting reviews in advance and evaluating work through other means.

[Four deans agreed, three disagreed, and three expressed varying shades of perplexed ambiguity.]

c)   Reviews are an essential, almost indispensable part of our promotion process.

[Administrators divided evenly on this one, with six agreeing, six opposing, and three straddling the fence with great decanal dexterity.]

V.   Affirmative Action cases sometimes require a neutral technique for comparing the records of women scholars with their peers to determine whether they are being discriminated against. One such technique, commonly employed, involves pairing scholars. Are you also aware of any quantitative scale assigning average relative values to academic books, articles, notes, and reviews, so that one can decide whether the average scholar with a book, for example, has accomplished more or less than (say) the average scholar with ten articles and/or twenty reviews? (I have reason to think that someone has indeed devised such a scale for Affirmative Action purposes, but cannot locate it.)

[Almost all deans recoiled from the thought of such quantitative evaluation, though one claimed to have heard of such a scale in use at some midwestern university. Like alligators in the New York sewers, this scale may be only an academic myth serving deep-seated needs of *homo academicus*. One is reminded of the legendary professor, despised by students when he taught them but revered by them after graduation when they came to realize his true worth, who inevitably surfaces in faculty discussions of teaching evaluation, exercising much the same hold upon the academic imagination as the Wandering Jew does upon that of Western Christendom. But if such a scale exists, I for one would be curious to learn how its author characterized the relative values of the average book, article, note, and review.]

Notes

1. Paul West, "The Twilight Double-Header: Some Ambivalences of the Reviewer Reviewed," in *Directions in Literary Criticism: Contemporary Approaches to Literature*, ed. Stanley Weintraub and Philip Young (University Park: Pennsylvania State Univ. Press, 1973), p. 260.
2. Quoted by Karen J. Winkler, "With Fewer Reviews in Newspapers, Academic Books Found Harder to Sell," *Chronicle of Higher Education*, vol. 27, no. 17 (4 Jan. 1984):7.
3. Wolper, " 'A grass-blade': On Academic Reviewing," *Scholarly Publishing* 10 (1979):327.
4. George Woodcock, "The Critic as Mediator," *Scholarly Publishing* 4 (1973):208.
5. William McPherson, "The Book Reviewer's Craft," in *Book Reviewing*, ed. Sylvia Kamerman (Boston: The Writer, 1978), p. 72. Other quotations from articles in *Book Reviewing* are given page citations in the text. In their chapter "Book Reviewing," Lewis A. Coser, Charles Kadushin, and Walter W. Powell, *Books: The Culture and Commerce of Publishing* (New York: Basic Books, 1982), pp. 308–32, note this tendency in hack reviewing and offer much perceptive analysis of the reviewer's role. See also David Shaw's illuminating series of articles for the *Los Angeles Times*, "Reviewing Books: It's Haphazard" (11 Dec. 1985), "Fear, Power of N.Y. Times Book Review" (12 Dec. 1985), and "Choosing the Best of the Book Reviews" (13 Dec. 1985). On the history of journalistic logrolling see esp. William Charvat, "James T. Fields and the Beginnings of Book Promotion, 1840–1855," in *The Profession of Authorship in America, 1800–1870* (Columbus: Ohio State Univ. Press, 1968), pp. 168–89.

6. Woolf, *Reviewing, with a Note by Leonard Woolf* (1939 ; rpt. Folcroft, Pa.: Folcroft Press, 1969), p. 13.

7. About his correspondence with Hans Aarsleff, Gura wishes me to include the following comment: "What I sought to convey in my letter to you is that one of the country's foremost historians of language study knew what I was up to and approved of the work as it appeared—indeed, that we had written at length to each other about the book's contents. Your comment assumes, without good reason, that after I was alerted to other language theorists I did not consult them first-hand. In fact, I made conscious decisions to restrict the subject matter of the book after hearing from scholars like Aarsleff and looking into the individuals mentioned" (Philip Gura to Michael West, 9 January 1984). But my comment does not assume that he failed to consult at first hand whatever figures were specifically mentioned by Aarsleff. It assumes that he failed to investigate a *category* of material ("such material," of which Aarsleff gave him some specific examples) closely enough to grasp the relevance to Thoreau of other such figures specifically mentioned in my review. And that assumption I still take to be true.

8. Booth, "Three Functions of Reviewing at the Present Time," *Bulletin of the Midwest Modern Language Association* 11 (Spring 1978):2.

9. Blum, "Literary Lotto," *New York Magazine*, vol. 18, no. 3 (21 Jan. 1985):40.

10. Esslin, "On Being Reviewed," *Bulletin of the Midwest Modern Language Association* 11 (Spring 1978):20–21.

Contributors

RICHARD D. ALTICK is Regents Professor of English at the Ohio State University.

RALPH COHEN is Kenan Professor of English at the University of Virginia and editor of *New Literary History*.

ANGUS EASSON is Professor of English at the University of Salford.

BRUCE D. MACPHAIL was marketing manager of the University of Oklahoma Press from 1979 until 1981.

ROBERT L. PATTEN is Professor of English at Rice University. He founded *Dickens Studies Newsletter* (now *Dickens Quarterly*) in 1970, and from 1978 until 1984 he edited *SEL: Studies in English Literature, 1500–1900*.

DEREK PEARSALL is Professor of English at the University of York.

STANLEY WEINTRAUB is Professor of English and Director of the Institute for the Arts and Humanistic Studies at the Pennsylvania State University.

JAMES L. W. WEST III is Professor of English at the Pennsylvania State University and co-editor of *Review*.

MICHAEL WEST is Professor of English at the University of Pittsburgh.